TIME FOR KIDS

BIG
BOOK OF
WHY

ACTIVITY BOOK

Written by Cari Jackson

Editor, TIME For Kids: Nellie Gonzalez Cutler
Senior Editor, TIME For Kids: Brenda Iasevoli

LIBERTY
STREET

Writer: Cari Jackson
Executive Editor: Beth Sutinis
Editor: Deirdre Langeland
Art Director: Georgia Morrissey
Designer: Penny Lamprell
Production Manager: Hillary Leary
Prepress Manager: Alex Voznesenskiy

© 2017 Time Inc. Books

Published by Liberty Street, an imprint of Time Inc. Books
225 Liberty Street
New York, NY 10281

LIBERTY STREET and TIME FOR KIDS are trademarks of Time Inc.

All rights reserved. No part of this book my be reproduced in any form or by any electronic or mechanical means, including information storage and retrieval systems, without permission in writing from the publisher, except by a reviewer, who may quote brief passages in a review.

ISBN: 978-1-68330-757-0

First Edition, 2017
1 QGS 17
1 3 5 7 9 8 6 4 2

We welcome your comments and
suggestions about Time Inc. Books.
Please write to us at:
Time Inc. Books
Attention: Book Editors
P.O. Box 62310
Tampa, FL 33662-2310
(800) 765-6400

timeincbooks.com

Time Inc. Books products may be purchased for business or promotional use. For information on bulk purchases, please contact Christi Crowley in the Special Sales Department at (845) 895-9858.

Contents

Each page in this book answers big questions about how the world works. The activities are fun, challenging, and full of information. The book is divided into sections by subject—you can read straight through from beginning to end, or jump to a section that interests you.

Animals

Wildlife can be as cute as a kitten or as deadly as a cobra. Supersmart elephants, crows, and dolphins can work as a team and solve complex puzzles, while eagles, tigers, and bears survive thanks to their speed and strength.

Why do wolves and dogs look so much alike?

Dog

Wolf

Scientists say that dogs evolved from wolves thousands of years ago. When they compared dog and wolf DNA, they found that every dog—from a Chihuahua to a Great Dane—is descended from wolves.

Why is this praying mantis throwing his hands up in the air like he just doesn't care?

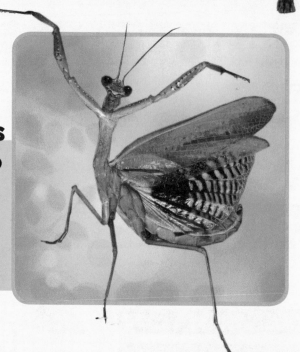

He is dancing to attract a mate.

FUNNY FILL-IN

Without looking at the rest of the sentence, fill in each blank with the type of word listed below it. Then read the whole story out loud to find out how silly it is.

Dozer the Marathon Dog (based on a TRUE story!)

Dozer, the _____ dog, saw a bunch of_____run by his house.
       adjective   plural noun

He became so_____that he_____the _____
           adjective   verb (past tense)   noun

and started to_____with them. _____miles later, Dozer_____
     verb (present tense)   number   verb (past tense)

across the finish line of the charity run. He_____ home the next day,
                                  verb (past tense)

looking so_____that his _____ took him to the vet. Word
         adjective   noun

got around, and they realized Dozer was the dog on the _____.
                                             noun

Marathon organizers gave Dozer a _____. Now he has his own
                           noun

_____—and he _____ to _____
   noun   verb ending in "s"   verb

money for a cancer center!

What makes apes and monkeys different?

All apes and monkeys belong to a group of animals called primates, but they differ in several ways. Apes don't have tails, but most monkeys do. Monkeys mostly run across the tops of tree branches, while apes have strong, broad shoulders that allow them to swing from branch to branch. Apes have bigger brains than monkeys do and can use tools, such as sticks and rocks.

Which is which?

For each picture below, see if you can figure out whether the animal is an ape or a monkey. Write your answer on the line below.

Did you know ?

Orangutans spend almost all of their time in trees. They live in rain forests on two islands in Indonesia, but humans are destroying their habitat for farming. Without our help, orangutans could be the first apes to go extinct.

Why don't bats get dizzy hanging upside down?

When we hang upside down, blood rushes to our heads, which makes us dizzy. But bats are so lightweight that gravity doesn't affect their blood flow. Bats have special tendons in their feet that help them hang—even when they're asleep.

CONNECT THE DOTS

Who's hanging around? Connect the dots to find out.

By the Numbers
Bats can eat more than 1,000 mosquitoes in an hour.

Why can't a fish breathe when out of water?

Fish and humans need oxygen to live. Humans have lungs to absorb oxygen from the air, while fish have gills to take in oxygen from water. Here's how it works. Fish gulp water that passes through their gills. Tiny blood vessels in the gills absorb oxygen that is mixed in with the water. So, a fish out of water is like a human without air.

Boesman's rainbowfish live in Indonesia.

COLOR IT IN

See how many colors you can use to color in this fish.

Tell me a joke

Q: Which part of a fish weighs the most?

A: Its scales!

How are crocodiles and alligators different?

Crocodiles and alligators belong to a group of reptiles called crocodilians. Alligators have wide, rounded snouts. Crocodile snouts are more pointed. Crocodiles prefer saltwater habitats, and alligators prefer freshwater. Alligators live only in the U.S. and China. Crocodiles can be found in Central and South America, Africa, Southeast Asia, and Australia.

Crocodile

Alligator

SPOT THE DIFFERENCE

Which of these crocodiles isn't like the others? Circle your choice.

! This may surprise you . . .

Alligators are actually great climbers. They'll climb onto a perch in a tree to sunbathe.

By the Numbers

Crocodile and alligator mothers can gently carry up to 15 babies in their mouths. Babies stay with their mothers for the first two years of life.

How are cats able to get what they want from us?

When cats want food, they meow in the same frequency range as a baby's cry. Humans find the sound difficult to ignore. Hungry cats will also dart between their owners' legs to steer them in the direction of food.

 Scaredy Cat

Draw three things Scaredy Cat is afraid of.

 **Cuddly Cat**

Draw three things Cuddly Cat loves.

CROSSWORD

Complete the puzzle by filling in a word that fits each clue. Write one letter per square.

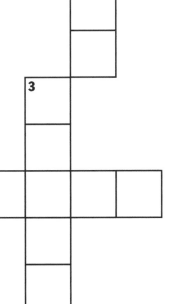

How do horses communicate?

Horses whinny and neigh when they meet or leave each other. They snort to warn others of danger. Stallions (male horses) roar as a mating call. Mares (female horses) whicker, or make a deep, smooth neigh, when they are nursing a foal (baby horse).

CHAMPION

Across

2. A deep, smooth neighing sound
5. Adult female horse
6. Infant horse

Down

1. A group of horses that live together
3. Adult male horse

Why do ants live in large colonies?

An ant colony can be home to hundreds of thousands of ants. Most ants have a job to do, such as guarding the nest, tending to the young, or gathering food. There is only one queen. Living and working together increases the ants' chances of survival.

Did you know ?

Formica ants use twigs to build massive domes over their underground nests. The dome can reach nearly five feet tall.

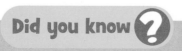

Formica ant hill

Get this ant to bed!

Help this ant find its way to a good night's sleep after a hard day's work.

Why can birds fly?

Birds have many physical features that make flight possible. They have light, streamlined bodies, with hollow bones. Strong breast muscles flap wings and propel birds forward and up. Smooth, light feathers reduce weight and drag.

MATCHING

Write the name of each bird on the lines beneath its picture.

Bald Eagle
Barn Owl
Blue Jay
Cardinal
Pelican
Raven
Robin
Sparrow
Starling

_ _ _ _ _

_ _ _ _   _ _ _ _ _

_ _ _ _ _ _ _ _

_ _ _ _ _
_ _ _

_ _ _ _ _

_ _ _ _ _ _ _ _ _

_ _ _ _ _ _ _ _ _

_ _ _ _ _ _ _ _ _

_ _ _ _ _
_ _ _

Why do bees make honey?

Honey is food for bees. To make the sticky stuff, honeybees gather nectar, a sweet liquid produced by flowers. Back at the hive, they transfer the liquid into honeycomb cells. Then they flap their wings until the liquid thickens. Now the honeybees have plenty of tasty honey.

By the Numbers
As many as 70,000 bees can live in one hive.

Did you know ?

Bees also produce special wax, called beeswax, that can be used to make products such as candles, soap, and cosmetics.

! This may surprise you . . .

When bees find a good source of nectar, they perform a dance to let other bees in the hive know how to get there.

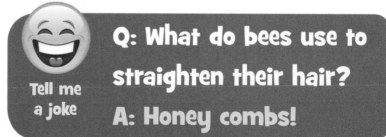

Tell me a joke

Q: What do bees use to straighten their hair?

A: Honey combs!

WORD SEARCH

It takes a whole lot of flowers, bees, and hard work to make a hive full of honey. Can you find all the words related to honey-making? Each of the words in the box below is hidden in the word search grid. The word might be forward, backward, or even diagonal. Spot and circle them all!

R	Q	N	E	A	N	J	I	E	K	C	I
F	T	E	T	C	E	L	L	O	C	S	R
I	R	R	G	A	M	T	E	A	J	E	P
N	F	S	A	B	A	I	T	C	W	E	H
A	A	H	N	N	T	L	B	O	S	D	N
Y	K	C	I	T	S	T	L	R	N	G	E
E	R	M	E	V	W	F	Z	T	L	L	L
M	A	O	K	L	E	J	O	G	B	I	L
D	T	O	C	H	E	D	U	R	P	T	O
C	C	L	E	T	T	O	Y	O	M	S	P
E	E	B	Y	E	N	O	H	W	P	I	B
R	N	H	A	K	T	F	S	U	M	P	W

Bloom	**Hive**	**Seed**
Collect	**Honeybee**	**Stamen**
Flower	**Nectar**	**Sticky**
Food	**Pistil**	**Sweet**
Grow	**Pollen**	**Transform**

Why do spiders spin webs?

Spiders spin webs mostly to catch insects. Golden orb spiders weave the largest and strongest webs. Their tightly woven nets catch small insects. Small birds sometimes get caught, but the golden orbs usually do not eat them. In fact, the spiders line barrier webs with insect husks to warn the birds away.

Golden orb spider

Match-Up

Circle the two spiderwebs that are the same.

Did you know ?

Newly hatched spiderlings quickly go off alone, because spider siblings have a bad habit of eating one another.

Spiderling

Why do some bugs glow in the dark?

Fireflies and other glow-in-the-dark bugs are bioluminescent (by-oh-loo-muh-NESS-ent). Chemicals in their bodies create energy in the form of light. Some fireflies light up to communicate with each other as they look for a mate. Others use their bioluminescence to warn predators or to lure prey.

ACROSTIC

In an acrostic poem, each line starts with a different letter from a word. Write your poem about fireflies on the lines below.

F _____

I _____

R _____

E _____

F _____

L _____

Y _____

Earth

Forces on Earth can cause mass destruction. Volcanoes spew molten lava. Earthquakes crack the land and douse coastlines with tsunamis. Clouds throw down vicious tornadoes and hurricanes. Yet, Earth also makes a comfy home for 8.7 million species of plants, animals, fungi, and microorganisms. Let's find out what makes this place so special.

Why is Earth a Goldilocks planet?

Our planet orbits in what scientists call the Goldilocks Zone. This is the distance from the sun where temperatures are not too hot or too cold to support life. Earth has water, a breathable atmosphere, and just the right amount of sunshine. Just like Baby Bear's porridge in the children's story "Goldilocks and the Three Bears," everything on Earth is "just right."

WORD SCRAMBLE

Unscramble the names of the continents, and then see
if you can match them to the continents on the map!

ARCIFA _ _ _ _ _ _

NATTIARACC _ _ _ _ _ _ _ _ _ _

OUEPRE _ _ _ _ _ _

ISAA _ _ _ _

NORHT CMAAIER _ _ _ _ _   _ _ _ _ _ _ _

SHUOT CMAAIER _ _ _ _ _   _ _ _ _ _ _ _

ATRSIAAUL _ _ _ _ _ _ _ _ _

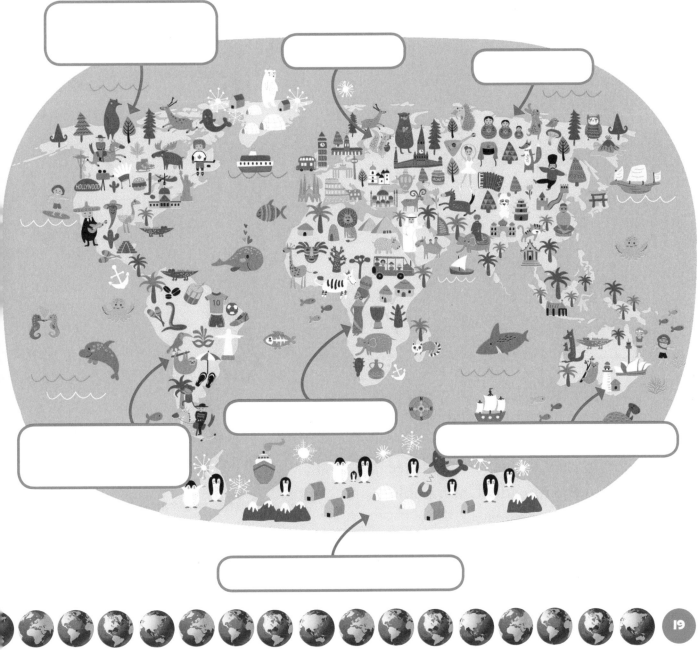

Why do tornadoes form?

Tornadoes form during powerful storms called supercells. Fast winds roll the air below the clouds into a horizontal spinning tube, or vortex. As warm air rises, it lifts the vortex into a vertical position. When the rotating cloud reaches down and touches the ground, it becomes a tornado.

Tornadoes have occurred in every U.S. state and on every continent except Antarctica.

A   O   R   D   D   O   N   A   Y   E

Word Scramble

What is the name of the region in the United States where most tornadoes occur? We've rescued three letters from the tornado. Unscramble the rest to reveal the answer.

T _ _ _ _ _ _ _   _ L L _ _

The fastest wind speed ever recorded was 318 miles per hour. It was measured in Oklahoma on May 13, 1999.

Why do volcanoes erupt?

Look at the picture next to the blanks to figure out what words belong there. Fill in all the blanks to read about volcanic eruptions.

Imagine a _ _ _ d _ _ _ _ _ _ . Shake it, and _g_ _ _ and pressure

build up inside. Open the top and—bam!—an _ _ _ _ _ p _l_ _ _ _ _ _

occurs. _ _ _l_ _ _ n _ _ _ _ work the same way. The _ _h_ _ _ _

deep inside _ _ _ r _ _ _ is so intense that it melts _ _ o _ _ _

and creates explosive _g_ _ _ _ _s_ . Scientists call that molten rock

magma. Magma slowly rises to the surface, collecting in underground chambers.

Eventually, the pressure of the magma becomes so great that it pushes through

Earth's _ _ _ _ u _ _ _ . Soon a _ _ _ _ l _ _ _ _ _ is blowing its top.

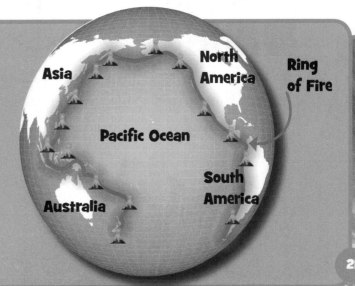

By the Numbers

There are more than 1,500 active volcanoes on Earth. More than 75 percent are located in the Ring of Fire, along the edges of the Pacific Ocean.

Asia

North America

Ring of Fire

Pacific Ocean

South America

Australia

Why is it so hot at the Grand Canyon?

There's very little moisture in the air to filter the sun's rays before they reach the ground, so the canyon is often hotter than 100 degrees. Unprepared visitors can overheat and experience impaired vision.

Check out these optical illusions and tell us what you see.

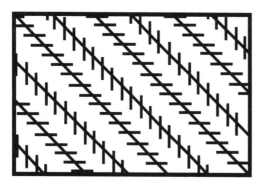

Are the long black lines parallel to (even with) one another, or are they crooked?

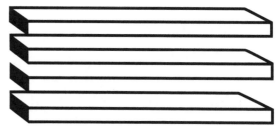

How many planks do you see?

What do you see where the white lines cross?

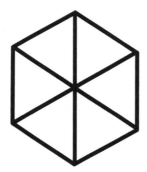

Is this a hexagon—or can you see something else?

By the Numbers

In the Grand Canyon, the Colorado River cuts through rock that is 1.75 billion years old.

22

Why does the earth shake during an earthquake?

Earthquakes happen when two giant pieces of the earth's crust press really hard against each other. Pressure builds up until—*crack!*—the pieces slip.

WORD SEARCH

Can you find the words related to these big Earth events? Each of the words in the box below is hidden in the word search grid. The word might be forward, backward, or even diagonal. Spot and circle them all!

W	I	N	D	V	D	E	O	M	S	N
M	P	O	R	W	K	C	S	T	N	F
L	O	T	V	A	B	V	L	C	B	C
L	U	S	H	I	E	A	E	R	E	I
C	E	S	T	Q	H	M	D	U	Q	M
R	N	O	W	U	Z	T	I	S	N	S
A	G	V	I	O	L	E	N	T	V	I
C	Y	X	S	A	X	U	S	Q	P	E
K	F	S	T	R	E	N	G	T	H	S
R	E	N	E	R	G	Y	N	G	C	A
S	T	O	R	M	S	U	R	G	E	X

Crack

Crust

Energy

Seismic

Shake

Storm

Strength

Surge

Twister

Violent

Wind

Why do clouds form?

Clouds form when warm, moist air rises from the earth. The water vapor cools as it rises and condenses into droplets, forming a cloud.

A thunderhead cloud can hold more than 2 billion pounds of water.

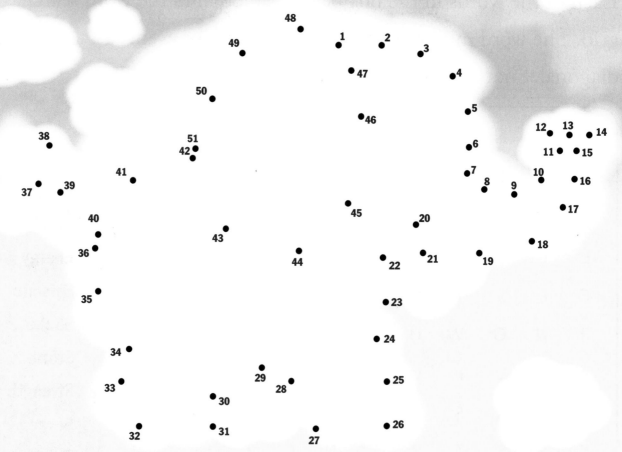

DOT-TO-DOT

Have you ever looked up and seen a face, or a ship, or a herd of horses in the clouds? Connect the dots to reveal the image in the clouds.

ACROSTIC

In an acrostic poem, each line starts with a different letter from a word. Write a poem about a tsunami (a giant ocean wave) below.

T _____

S _____

U _____

N _____

A _____

M _____

I _____

Why does the ocean have waves?

Most waves are caused by wind. Energy from the wind transfers to the water through friction. The waves transmit the energy. Unless something (such as a coastline) stops the wave, it can travel across the entire ocean basin.

Why is Earth's climate changing?

In a word: humans. Factories, cars, engines, and other machines spew a lot of pollution that builds up inside our atmosphere. Normally, the sun's rays bounce off the earth and go back into space. But human-made particles and gasses trap the sun's heat, causing temperatures to rise. Scientists have been trying to warn us: Make changes—fast—or things will get worse.

What are the signs of climate change?

- Changing rain and snow patterns
- Stronger storms
- Heat waves
- Damaged coral reefs
- Warmer oceans
- Rising sea levels
- More droughts and wildfires
- Less snow and ice
- Changes in plant life cycles

Did you know ?

Climate change is causing Isle de Jean Charles, Louisiana, to sink into the sea. Residents have had to leave their homes.

Please help me!

ENERGY QUIZ

Can you spot the wasteful habits? For each picture below, check the green box if it shows a behavior that is good for the environment, or the red box if the behavior is wasteful.

 ○ ○    ○ ○    ○ ○    ○ ○

 ○ ○    ○ ○    ○ ○    ○ ○

 ○ ○    ○ ○    ○ ○

 ○ ○    ○ ○

Look around your own house. What can your family do to conserve energy?

Why do people sink in quicksand?

In quicksand, there is more water (or air) between the grains of sand than there is actual sand. The grain structure is stacked so that the "ground" holds up—unless something heavy, like a passing person, pushes on it. Then the sand grains collapse, making a space that the object can fall into. The best way to get out of quicksand is to relax, lie on your back, and slowly pull yourself out of the mess.

How are Earth's rocks grouped?

All the rocks on Earth fall into one of three categories: igneous, sedimentary, or metamorphic.

Igneous rocks, **such as pumice, form when molten rock reaches Earth's surface and cools.**

Sedimentary rocks, **such as sandstone, form when sediments build up and are compacted together by Earth's powerful forces.**

Metamorphic rocks, **such as marble, are created when igneous or sedimentary rock changes, or metamorphoses, as a result of temperature, pressure, or stress.**

FUNNY FILL-IN

Without looking at the rest of the sentence, fill in each blank with the type of word listed below it. Then read the whole story to find out how silly it is.

The Worst Kayaking Trip Ever

It was a _____ day in the middle of _____. I woke up feeling
             adjective   season

_____. My buddy Nick and I planned to go kayaking on the river near
   emotion

our house. I put on my _____ and _____ to meet my
                        piece of clothing   verb (past tense)

friend at the boat launch. We _____ with the current. We paddled
                              verb (past tense)

around a _____ and almost hit a _____. Finally, we got
            noun   noun

_____ and _____ to the bank. I stepped one foot onto the
  adjective   verb (past tense)

sandy bank and _____ sank up to my _____. Quicksand!
                 adverb   part of body

It held me like _____. "Don't _____!" Nick hollered.
                  noun   verb (present tense)

The more I _____, the more I sank. Nick held out a _____ and
             verb (past tense)   noun

I grabbed on. He _____ and _____, and finally, I was free!
                  verb (past tense)   same verb

But I smelled like _____. We _____ back home. It was
                     noun   verb (past tense)

the _____ kayaking trip ever.
      adjective ending in "est"

Why is the atmosphere important?

Earth is surrounded by several layers of gases. This atmosphere works as a blanket to keep the planet warm, trapping some of the sun's warmth close to the surface. The outer layers also protect us from the sun's harmful rays.

DRAW YOUR OWN

Humans cause most of the air pollution on our planet. But you can reduce the amount of greenhouse gases that you create! Draw yourself traveling in an environmentally friendly way, such as riding a bus, a commuter train, a bike, or a skateboard—or just walking!

Mesosphere
The layer that burns up most meteors before they can hit Earth!

Stratosphere
Where the ozone layer is located. Ozone absorbs harmful ultraviolet rays.

ozone

Troposphere
Where we live and where most weather happens.

31 miles (50 km) to 53 miles (85 km)

9 miles (14 km) to 31 miles (50 km)

up to 9 miles (14 km) above sea level

Why is the ocean salty?

Ocean water gets its salt from rocks on land. Rain contains a small amount of carbon dioxide, which causes the rainwater to be slightly acidic. When rain falls on rocks, the acidity breaks down the rock and carries salt and minerals through rivers to the ocean.

Did you know ?

The more salt in the water, the denser, or thicker, it gets. That's why it's easier to float in salt water than in freshwater.

What floats, and what sinks?

Draw a squiggly water line at the bottom of each item that floats. Draw an arrow pointing down on each item that sinks.

A dense plastic toy may sink, but a lighter or hollow plastic toy will float. Try out a few and see what happens!

Space

Space is the place that begins about 60 miles above our planet. There, the air is so thin that no one can breathe. Outside the earth's atmosphere, astronauts have little protection against the sun's radiation. Despite the challenges, humans still dream of exploring our galaxy.

You can see part of our galaxy, the Milky Way, at night.

Why does Earth have a moon?

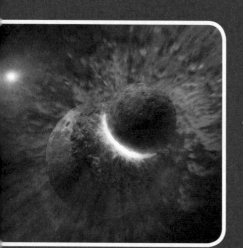

About 4.5 million years ago, just a little while after Earth was born, a Mars-sized object crashed into our planet. A huge chunk of Earth flew into outer space.

Did you know ❓

Asteroids and meteoroids often smash into the moon's surface, forming craters.

❗ This may surprise you . . .

During a total lunar eclipse, Earth's shadow covers the moon. The filtered light causes the moon to take on a reddish color, creating what some people call a blood moon.

CROSSWORD

Complete the puzzle by filling in a word that fits each clue. Write one letter per square.

Across

2. The _____ of the moon is powdery.
3. When you fall, blame this.
5. A lunar eclipse that turns the moon red is a ____ moon.
7. Asteroids cause these.
8. When the moon enters Earth's shadow
9. It's always at your feet.

Down

1. Related to the moon
4. Get a close-up view with this.
6. The stars at night are big and ____.

Get a close-up view with this.

Why are space rockets so fast?

To leave Earth's atmosphere and travel 60 miles (96 km) to space, rockets have to fight the mighty force of gravity. The speed to accomplish that—called escape velocity—is calculated for each size and type of rocket. A rocket launching a space shuttle needs to reach 7 miles per second (11km per second).

Space race!

Get your space mission to launch first! Roll one die, and move your game piece the right number of spaces. Play with a friend and see who finishes first.

You'll need: dice and game pieces or coins.

Start **T-43 hours and counting**

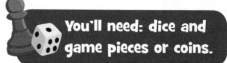

A scientific instrument isn't working. Back one space.

T Minus means the time before the launch.

Yikes! Hydrogen gas leak! Back one space.

You passed the booster test! Move ahead three spaces.

Storm in the Atlantic delays launch. Back one space.

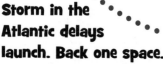

T-0 Solid rocket booster ignition and liftoff!

Finish

Why do people live on the International Space Station (ISS)?

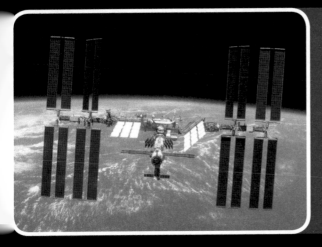

Astronauts on the ISS perform experiments and study the human body's reactions to weightlessness. The ISS orbits 249 miles (400 km) above Earth. It travels 17,899 miles per hour (28,800 km/h), completing a loop around Earth every 90 minutes.

MAZE

Time to return to your family on Earth. Find your path back home.

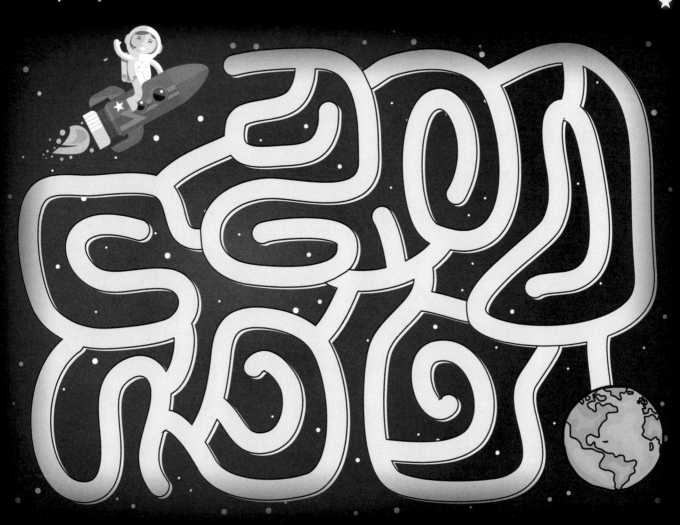

Why is a manned mission to Mars so dangerous?

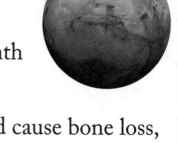

Astronauts would face many dangers on the six-month trek to Mars. Exposure to the sun's radiation would increase astronauts' risk for cancer. Low gravity could cause bone loss, vision problems, and muscle weakness. And being confined to a small space far from home can cause stress.

WORD SEARCH

Search up, down, forward, and backward.

R	A	D	S	T	Q	G	W	E	G	Z
V	T	R	U	V	S	R	X	I	Q	O
R	W	C	N	A	S	A	C	R	N	L
A	E	E	M	L	H	V	H	O	O	Y
R	A	D	I	A	T	I	O	N	S	M
S	H	U	S	G	U	T	P	O	S	P
T	O	L	S	G	H	Y	T	X	S	U
B	C	A	I	R	A	T	L	I	I	S
S	W	H	O	I	O	P	L	D	M	M
K	C	A	N	Y	O	N	U	E	U	O
V	P	O	M	V	S	T	R	A	S	N
T	U	A	N	O	R	T	S	A	X	S

Astronaut
Canyon
Gravity
Iron Oxide
Mission
NASA
Olympus Mons
Radiation
Weightless

CRYPTOGRAM

Each letter in a cryptogram stands for another letter. Fill in the names on the solar system chart below. Once you've found the real letters that correspond with each code letter, fill in the key to solve.

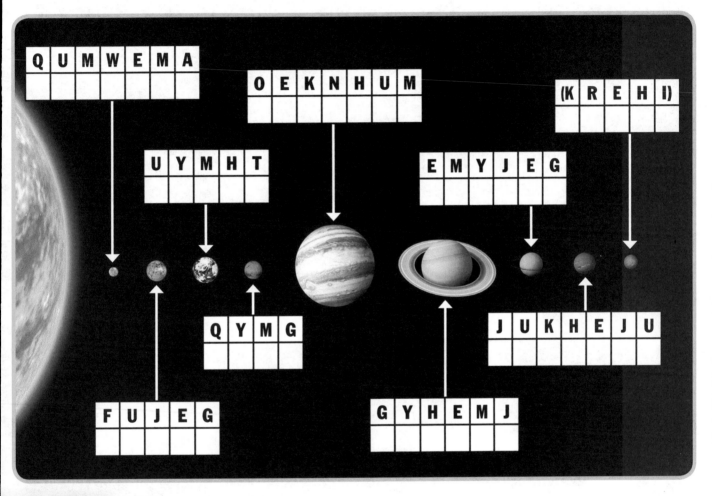

| Q | U | M | W | E | M | A |
| | | | | | | |

| O | E | K | N | H | U | M |
| | | | | | | |

| (K | R | E | H | I) |
| | | | | |

| U | Y | M | H | T |
| | | | | |

| E | M | Y | J | E | G |
| | | | | | |

| Q | Y | M | G |
| | | | |

| J | U | K | H | E | J | U |
| | | | | | | |

| F | U | J | E | G |
| | | | | |

| G | Y | H | E | M | J |
| | | | | | |

KEY

A	B	C	D	E	F	G	H	I	J	K	L	M	N	O	P	Q	R	S	T	U	V	W	X	Y	Z
Z	W	X								Q					K	M		G				F		D	B

Earth is not too close and not too far from the sun.

Use your key to find the name for this type of planet:

| S | I | R | X | N | R | I | W | P | G | | K | R | Y | J | U | H |
| | | | | | | | | | | | | | | | | |

Why don't planets orbit in perfect circles?

Planets travel around the sun in elliptical, or oval-like, orbits. Gravity pulls the planets toward the sun, while each planet's forward momentum tries to keep it moving in a straight line. This tug-of-war causes an elliptical orbit.

The Milky Way

CROSSWORD

You are here.

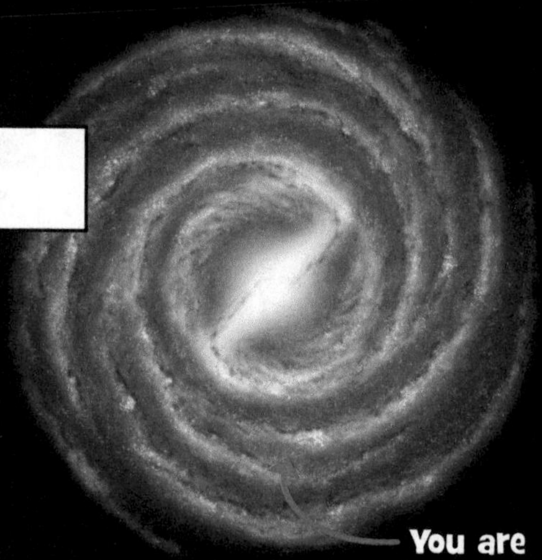

Across

2. The force that pulls planets toward the sun
4. To turn on an axis
5. The shape of a planet's orbit
6. The center of the solar system

Down

1. The path that Earth travels around the sun
3. The force that moves us forward

Why do astronomers measure distances in light-years?

Outer space is too vast to measure by miles and kilometers. Astronomers use light-years instead. A light-year is the distance light can travel in space in one year—roughly 5.88 trillion miles (9.46 trillion km).

SUDOKU ★

Fill the empty squares so that the numbers 1 to 9 appear only once in each row, column, and 3x3 box.

9	7	2			6	5		1
4	1	2	5	3	9	7	6	
	5	6	4	7	1	3	2	9
	8			9	5	6		7
6		9		4		2	1	
5	7	1	3	6	2		9	4
7	2		9	1	3	4		6
		3		5		9	7	2
9	4	5	6		7	1	8	

Did you know ❓

Our solar system is in orbit around the center of the Milky Way galaxy. It takes 230 million years for our solar system to complete one orbit.

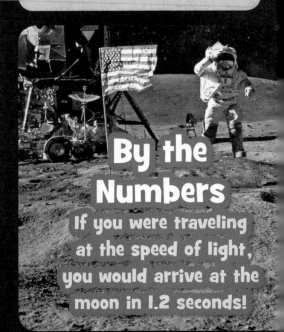

By the Numbers

If you were traveling at the speed of light, you would arrive at the moon in 1.2 seconds!

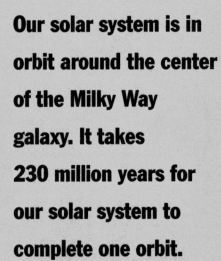

Why do galaxies have different shapes?

When billions of stars, planets, gas, and dust are held together by gravity, a galaxy forms. Galaxies come in three shapes: elliptical, spiral, and irregular. They are shaped by many different forces, including centrifugal force (which pushes objects on a circular path outward), collisions with other galaxies, and gravity. Our galaxy, the Milky Way, is a spiral galaxy.

Elliptical

Spiral

Irregular

By the Numbers

Our sun is one of 100 billion stars in the Milky Way galaxy. Some scientists think there could be as many as 100 billion galaxies in the universe.

Tell me a joke

Q: Why did the cow go to outer space?

A: To visit the Milky Way!

40

LOOK AND FIND

These spaceships are heading back to Earth, but one of them is bringing home an alien. Can you find it?

Why are comets so predictable?

A comet is like a big, dirty snowball, with a core of ice and dust. When a comet passes near the sun, some of the ice melts, creating a tail of gas and dust. Like planets, comets have consistent orbits around the sun. That's why scientists know that the famous Halley's Comet will pass Earth on July 28, 2061, for the first time in 75 years.

2061 JULY 28

WORD SCRAMBLE

Hint: There are millions of the first word in this answer.

Millions of asteroids orbit the sun in a region of our solar system located between Mars and Jupiter. Three letters have been filled in below. Unscramble the rest to find out what that region is called.

_ _ T _ O _ _ _ _ L _

Why isn't Pluto a planet anymore?

Pluto and its largest moon, Charon

Once upon a time, Pluto was a full-fledged planet. But a planet has to meet three criteria: it must orbit a sun, it must have enough mass that gravity shapes it into a sphere, and it has to have cleared away the other objects in its orbit. Pluto meets the first two criteria, but not the third.

A poem for Pluto

A concrete poem has an appearance that matches its topic. Think about how Pluto must feel out there in the cold darkness, as a dwarf planet. Then, write a poem about Pluto in the shape of its orbit around the sun.

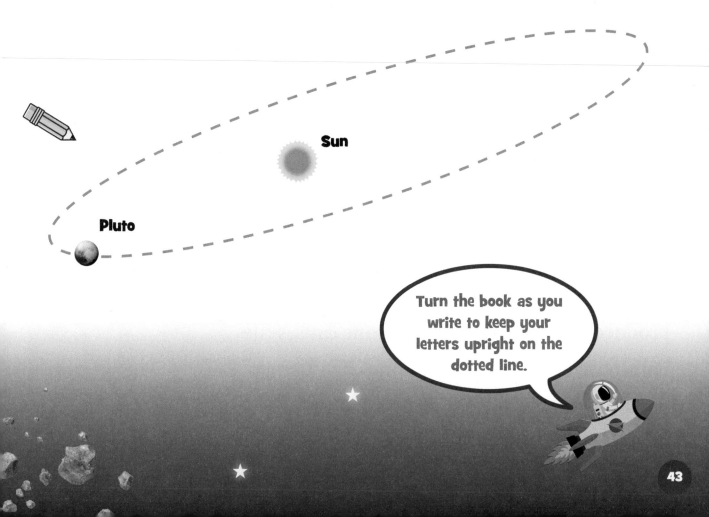

Sun

Pluto

Turn the book as you write to keep your letters upright on the dotted line.

Humans

How do humans work? Let's take a look at why we look the way we do and why we can do the things we can do. What makes us sick, and what keeps us healthy? Why do we sleep and what makes us laugh? Humans are not the only animals that have these amazing features, but we think we're pretty special.

By the Numbers
The average head has 100,000 hair follicles. Each follicle grows about 20 hairs in a lifetime.

Did you know ?

Kids learn through play! The United Nations named playtime a human right for every child. Play helps you grow strong, learn how to get along with others, and solve problems.

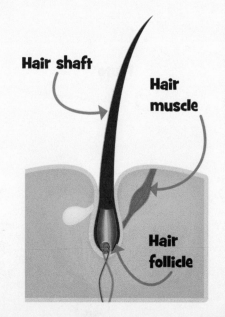

! This May Surprise You . . .

A tiny muscle is attached to every hair on your body. When you get cold or scared, your body produces adrenaline. This hormone causes the hair muscles to contract, holding each hair up straight. The result: goose bumps!

Hair shaft

Hair muscle

Hair follicle

Why are some hairs curly?

To understand why hair grows curly or straight, you need to go to the source: the hair follicle. A follicle is a sac under the skin from which hair grows. When follicles are asymmetrical, or uneven, they produce hair that is oval, causing the strand to curl. If the follicle is symmetrical, the strand is round and grows straight.

SQUIGGLE!

Draw a whole head of hair without lifting your pencil off the page!

How many hairs total does the average head grow in a lifetime?

Answer on page 123

Why are eyes different colors?

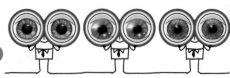

The color of your eyes depends on how much melanin you have. Melanin is a pigment, or a substance that creates color, that is produced by your body. Those who have a lot of melanin have brown eyes. Very little melanin creates blue eyes. Green eyes lie somewhere in between.

CROSSWORD

Complete the puzzle by filling in a word that fits each clue. Write one letter per square.

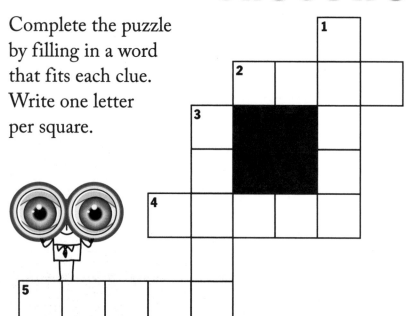

Across
2. Eyes with hardly any melanin are this color.
4. These pour out of tiny glands in our eyes.
5. Eyes with a lot of melanin turn this color.

Down
1. It's the special ingredient in your eye boogers.
3. Eyes that have a medium amount of melanin turn this color.

Why do we get crusty stuff in the corners of our eyes?

Eye boogers, gunk, sleep: call that crusty stuff what you want, but the real name is rheum (pronounced "room"). It's made up of mucus, oil, and skin cells that naturally seep from our eyes. As it dries overnight, it collects in the corners of our eyes.

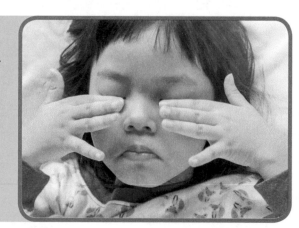

Why are some people color-blind?

Most people's eyes have retinas made up of small parts called cones and rods. Rods help people see in low light, while cones allow people to see objects in color. Each cone has a different pigment, which helps a person tell the difference between colors. But color-blind people are missing certain cones. So they might see colors, but not the right ones. Green vegetables might look brown, while red and green traffic lights look the same.

Color-blindness test

Can you see the number inside the circle?

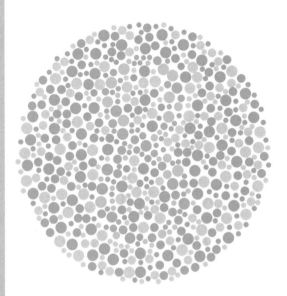

Why do we cry?

All tears come from tiny glands in the corner of each eye. But different tears serve different purposes. Basal tears clean our eyes and keep them moist. Reflex tears have more water to help clear the eye of irritants. Emotional tears release stress hormones, which may be why we usually feel better after a good cry!

Why do baby teeth fall out?

Teeth don't keep growing the way you do. As kids—and their jaws—grow, the teeth stay the same. Eventually, the baby teeth get pushed out to make room for the larger permanent teeth.

 WORD SEARCH

Can you find all the dental words in the box below? Search up, down, forward, backward, and on the diagonal.

Canine

Grind

Incisor

Jaw

Molar

Permanent

Premolar

Sharp

V	H	U	N	O	D	C	V	E	F	G
O	M	O	L	A	R	C	H	U	B	H
L	R	K	E	S	O	L	W	E	S	O
A	U	Z	R	H	S	O	J	A	W	U
M	O	V	C	O	I	S	B	X	L	S
V	N	G	C	A	C	T	X	A	J	H
P	E	R	M	A	N	E	N	T	L	A
E	S	I	P	U	I	I	H	L	O	R
A	S	N	S	R	Q	H	N	C	W	P
L	O	D	R	A	L	O	M	E	R	P
R	E	V	S	A	T	N	E	M	A	H

Why can we whistle?

Blowing air through your pursed lips causes the air to vibrate, which creates sound waves. Your mouth serves as a resonance chamber, much like the body of a guitar or violin, bouncing the sound waves around and making them louder.

CONNECT THE DOTS

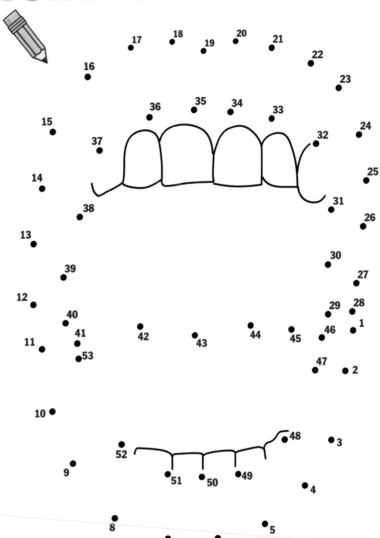

Did you know ?

Relative to its size, the tongue is the strongest muscle in the body. It is the only muscle that is attached just on one end.

Why are some people allergic to certain foods?

The body's immune system normally fights infection. But when someone is allergic to a food, the immune system thinks that food is dangerous. It releases chemicals called histamines to attack the "invader." The histamines cause symptoms such as coughing, rashes, stomachaches, and worse.

WORD SCRAMBLE

People can be allergic to almost any food, but most reactions are caused by these eight foods. Can you unscramble them all?

HSESLFILH _ _ _ _ _ _ _ _ _

SIFH _ _ _ _   LIMK _ _ _ _

REET SUTN _ _ _ _ _   _ _ _ _ _

TAHEW _ _ _ _ _   GEGS _ _ _ _

NEAPTUS _ _ _ _ _ _ _

YOS _ _ _

Why can broken bones fix themselves?

Bones are strong, but a hard fall can break them. Fortunately, bones are natural healers. Your body produces new cells and tiny blood vessels at the site of the break. The cells cover the broken area until they close up the break.

The human body has 206 bones. There are 26 bones in each foot, and 27 in each hand.

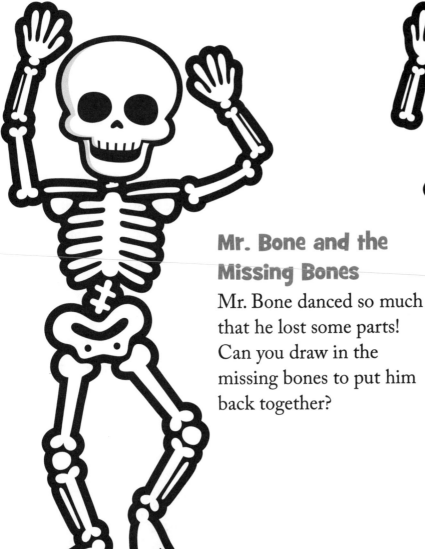

Mr. Bone and the Missing Bones

Mr. Bone danced so much that he lost some parts! Can you draw in the missing bones to put him back together?

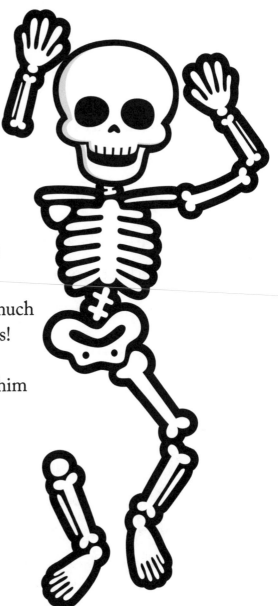

Why do we need sleep?

Scientists have a variety of theories about why we need sleep. One theory suggests that sleep allows the brain to process our memories from the day. Another theory is that sleep helps us conserve energy. Sleep may also allow us to repair and restore cells in our bodies overnight.

FIND THE MIX-UPS

A lack of sleep can make it difficult to concentrate, which can lead to poor grades! Sleep-deprived Jake did this writing assignment about his day. He scrambled letters and wrote some words totally wrong. Can you fix the mix-ups in each sentence?

1. Last night, I went to deb late.
2. I ate boatmeal for reakfast.
3. I forgot my munch at home.
4. My gym cheater told me to run faster.
5. I was rited by the end of the day.
6. I fell please in math class.
7. When I got home, I took a pan.

How much sleep do you need?*

Kids ages 6 to 13	9 to 11 hours
Teenagers ages 14 to 17	8 to 10 hours
Young adults ages 18 to 25	7 to 9 hours

*according to the National Sleep Foundation

Why are people ticklish?

Tickling stimulates nerve endings on sensitive parts of your body. A signal sent to the brain analyzes the touch. The instinct to laugh and squirm might be a way to teach ourselves self-defense. Tickling also helps parents connect with their babies.

MIX AND MATCH

These jokes (in red) and punch lines (in blue) are all mixed up. Draw a line to match the punch line to the joke. Then find a friend and share a few laughs!

Why do we need food?

Your body needs food the way a car needs gas. Food is your fuel: it gives you energy and nutrition to grow, move, and be healthy. Your body needs a balanced diet of fruits, grains, vegetables, dairy, and protein to get all the different nutrients it needs.

What is a calorie?

A calorie is a unit of measurement. The number of calories tells you how much energy your body will get from a serving of food or drink. Most school-age kids should get 1,600 to 2,200 calories per day.

Meal match

These plates are piled high with all the food groups. But only two have exactly the same foods on them. Can you find them?

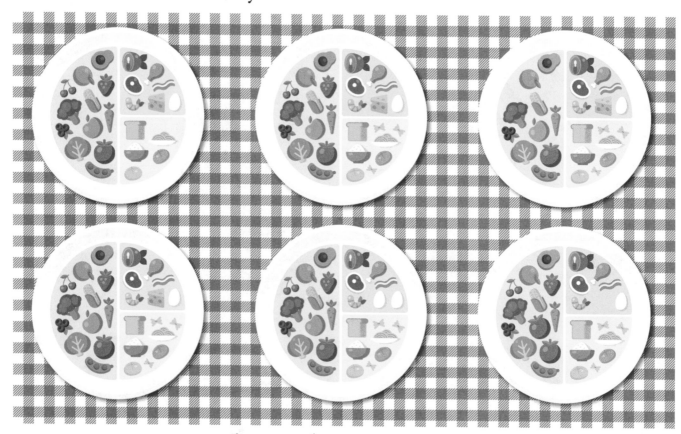

Why does chocolate make me hyper?

Chocolate contains sugar and caffeine. Caffeine sends a jolt to your nervous system and brain, making you more awake and alert. Meanwhile, the sugar goes into your bloodstream to provide a short burst of physical energy. Sugar also releases a chemical in your brain that makes you feel good.

ACROSTIC

Americans buy 58 million pounds of chocolate to demonstrate their love on Valentine's Day. A food so closely connected to love deserves a poem. Write your own acrostic poem, with each line of the poem starting with a letter from the word.

C _____

H _____

O _____

C _____

O _____

L _____

A _____

T _____

E _____

Why do some kids have freckles?

Melanin is a chemical produced by certain skin cells (melanocytes) to protect the skin from sun damage. The more melanin you have, the darker your skin. Sometimes melanin is produced in the skin in clumps instead of being evenly distributed. These clumps are freckles.

Why do people have different skin colors?

Everyone has about the same number of melanocytes, but not everyone produces the same amount of melanin. And that is why people have different skin colors.

Why are some people taller than others?

Height and other physical traits such as eye, hair, and skin color are passed down through genes from parents to children. Genes determine many things about you, including how much growth hormone your body produces and how big your bones get. Your diet, where you live, and your overall health also help decide how tall you'll be.

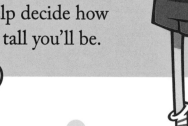

**Painting by
Georges Seurat**

Coloring with dots

Pointillism is a painting technique that uses tiny dots of color to form an image. The painter does not mix the dots of paint, but when the image is viewed at a distance, the colors in the dots appear to blend together. Use the pointillism dot technique to "paint" this scene with markers.

Around the World

The world is filled with amazing inventions, architectural wonders, and the occasional towering example of human error (we're looking at you, Pisa!). Take a tour of some dazzling buildings, engineering marvels, and wild expressions of culture. They all owe thanks to the human imagination.

The Burj Khalifa in Dubai stands at 2,716 feet (828 m), making it the world's tallest building.

Tower of Pisa

Did you know ?

Germans used the Tower of Pisa, in Italy, as a lookout in World War II. After the war, U.S. troops were ordered to demolish any German-held buildings. They stopped at the Tower. The Americans found it too charming and refused to bring it down.

Why is the Tower of Pisa leaning?

Poor planning led to the tilting of Italy's Tower of Pisa. The foundation of the 185-foot-tall (56.4-m) marble tower is a very shallow 10 feet (3.05 m). Plus, the whole tower stands on soft clay rather than sturdy bedrock. Within five years of the start of its construction in 1173, the structure began to sink on one side.

CAPTION THIS!

The wobbly posture of the Tower of Pisa has inspired plenty of jokes. Take a crack at writing the punch lines for this scene!

Why do so many people climb Mount Kilimanjaro?

Mount Kilimanjaro in Tanzania is Africa's tallest peak, topping out at 19,341 feet (5,895 m). Most mountains that tall are very dangerous to climb. Kilimanjaro's gentle slopes, however, make it possible for many people to reach the top. More than 40,000 people make the long walk each year. The youngest hiker to reach the top was only six years old!

World's top four highest peaks

Mount Everest, Nepal 29,029 feet (8,848 m)

K2, Pakistan 28,251 feet (8,611 m)

Aconcagua, Argentina 22,838 feet (6,961 m)

Denali, United States 20,310 feet (6,190 m)

Route to the top!

This hiker has a long way to go. Can you help him find the quickest route out of the mountains?

Why does the Golden Gate Bridge sway in the wind?

California's Golden Gate Bridge, which spans the entry to San Francisco Bay from the Pacific Ocean, can swing sideways up to 27 feet (8.23 m). The builder, Joseph Strauss, intentionally designed the 4,200-foot (1,280-m) center span of the bridge to sway in strong ocean winds. This keeps the bridge from collapsing from the pressure.

DRAW YOUR OWN

It's your turn to be the engineer. Draw a bridge across the river.

Why did France give the Statue of Liberty to the U.S.?

In 1865, French political thinker Edouard de Laboulaye wanted to give a statue to the United States as a sign of friendship. Democracy was still a new idea, and some people didn't like it. He hoped that the gift, named Liberty Enlightening the World, would inspire the French.

Statue of Liberty

DRAW YOUR OWN

Draw something new in the Statue of Liberty's hands, and add a speech bubble to create a cartoon.

WHERE IN THE WORLD?

Read the description of each statue below, then see if you can locate it on the world map. Write the number next to the statue in the correct circle.

1 Statue of Unity under construction in Gujarat, India
597 feet (182 m)

2 Spring Temple Buddha Henan, China
503 feet (153 m)

The Motherland Calls is the world's largest statue of a woman. (The Statue of Liberty only stands 151 feet without her base!)

3 Ushiku Daibutsu Ushiku, Japan
394 feet (120 m)

4 Statue of Liberty New York City, United States
305 feet (93 m)

5 The Motherland Calls Volgograd, Russia
279 feet (85 m)

6 Christ the Redeemer Rio de Janeiro, Brazil
132 feet (40 m)

Average two-story house=20 feet

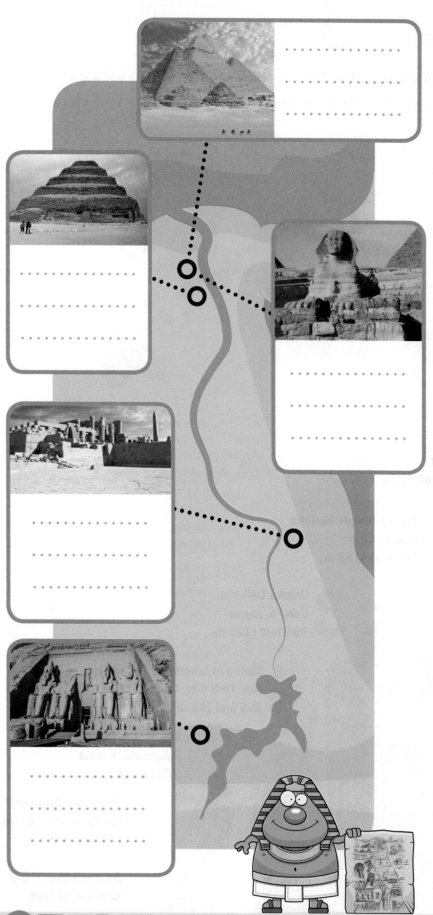

Monument match

Egypt is home to some of the great wonders of the ancient world. Use the clues in the column below to label these famous sites.

Abu Simbel
These temples built by King Ramses II include giant statues of himself and Egyptian gods.

Step-Pyramid at Saqqâra
In 2630 B.C., the famous architect Imhotep built the world's first major stone building as a funeral monument for King Djoser.

Great Sphinx of Giza
This massive half man and half lion statue lies at the foot of the Great Pyramid.

Temple of Karnak
Thirty different pharaohs added to the construction of the Temple of Karnak, the largest ancient religious site in the world.

Pyramids of Giza
These huge pyramids serve as tombs to three different pharaohs. The first and largest, called the Great Pyramid of Giza, was built in 2550 B.C.

Why is this building no longer a church?

The massive Hagia Sophia in Istanbul was built in 532 as a Catholic church. It was a symbol of the power of the Byzantine Empire. In 1453, the empire fell to an Ottoman sultan, who converted the building into a mosque. In 1934, the government of Turkey, which has no official religion, made it a museum.

COLOR IT IN

Color in the Hagia Sophia.

Why are Russian church domes shaped like onions?

Russian Orthodox churches have featured onion domes for more than 1,000 years. The shape is thought to evoke the curving flame of a candle. The interior framework, similar to a birdcage, gives the dome its shape. The domes are then covered in colorful metal.

A

B

C

D

E

F

Find the missing puzzle pieces

Three of the pieces on the left fit into the puzzle. Write the letter for the puzzle pieces that fit in the space where they belong.

What is Australia's nickname?

We've filled in a few letters to get you started. Read on to get some hints, and then fill in the rest!

T _ E   _ A _ _

D _ _ _   _ _ _ D _ R

When Europeans started going south to Australia, they felt the land was at the bottom of the world. Australia is below the equator, and "down under" just about everything on the European world map. That's how it ended up with this nickname.

Why does this Aboriginal musical instrument depend on termites?

Aborigines, the people who first settled in Australia at least 40,000 years ago, have been playing the didgeridoo, an eerie-sounding tubular instrument, for centuries. The best didgeridoos are made from eucalyptus trees that have been hollowed out by termites. The termites' tunnel patterns create a unique sound for each instrument.

Why was this ancient place called the Forbidden City?

In the middle of Beijing, the capital of China, sits a fortress that was once the imperial palace. This area, built between 1406 and 1420, served as the political center of the country for more than 500 years. Only the royal family could enter without special permission.

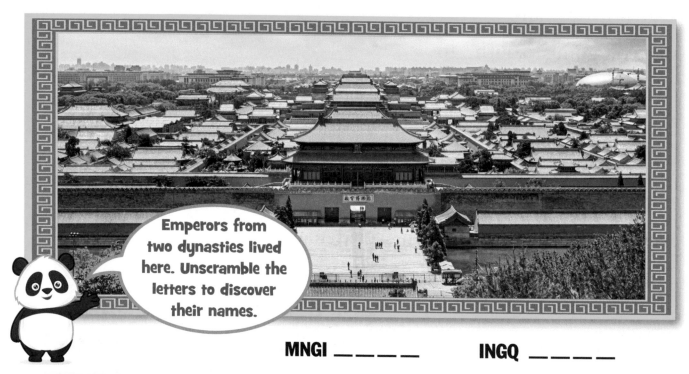

Emperors from two dynasties lived here. Unscramble the letters to discover their names.

MNGI _ _ _ _   INGQ _ _ _ _

! This may surprise you . . .

Chinese emperor Qin Shi Huang Di (born 259 B.C.) ordered an army of thousands of life-size clay soldiers to protect him in the afterlife. They were buried with him in 210 B.C. A group of farmers discovered these Terra Cotta Warriors while they were digging a well in 1974.

Why do people in Japan celebrate cherry blossoms?

Light pink, cloudlike cherry blossoms are a symbolic flower of spring, a time of renewal. The blossoms last only for a couple of weeks, symbolizing the fleeting nature of life. In Japan, people gather for picnics under the trees, a custom called Hanami. *Hanami* means "watching blossoms." Children in Japan start school near this time because it is seen as the natural new start of the year.

SPOT THE DIFFERENCE

These families have gathered for Hanami. Can you find eight differences in the pictures?

Giant tortoise

Blue-footed Booby

Why are the Galápagos Islands unique?

Darwin's finch

The Galápagos Islands are located 600 miles (966 km) off the coast of Ecuador. They are home to unusual plant and animal life found nowhere else on Earth. Marine iguanas, blue-footed boobies, giant tortoises, and more all call the Galápagos home. The island wildlife inspired Charles Darwin's theory of evolution.

Why are these giant statues on Easter Island?

The short answer is: no one knows! Easter Island is isolated in the South Pacific, 1,100 miles (1,770 km) from the nearest island. Polynesian voyagers landed here in 800 to 1200 A.D. In a few hundred years, they managed to clear all the trees (not so great) and create 1,000 giant Moai statues (pretty impressive). The 13-foot-tall, 14-ton heads all face the center of the island.

Make a face!

Draw the face on the Moai.

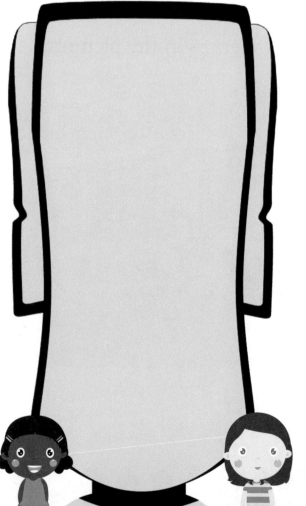

FUNNY FILL-IN

Without looking at the rest of the sentence, fill in each blank with the type of word listed below it. Then read the whole story out loud to find out how silly it is.

Gallivanting in the Galápagos

My family and I are taking a vacation at the Galápagos Islands. We know we have

to be _____ to protect the wildlife here. But it isn't easy with our
       adjective

_____ family! As my brother _____ to get a better view
adjective   verb (ending in s)

of a Darwin's finch, he nearly_____on a land iguana. The iguana
               verb (ending in s)

_____, which makes my dad _____ his _____ .
verb (ending in s)   verb   noun

Later, we _____ with sea lions and marine iguanas. One sea lion
       verb

_____ with a marine iguana. The marine iguana gets _____
verb (ending in s)   emotion

and _____ away. On the last day, we watch blue-footed boobies
   verb (ending in s)

_____ to show off their _____ blue feet. Finally, we
    verb   adjective

_____ our _____ and get ready to _____ home.
  verb   noun   verb

Why are there so many cowboys in Argentina?

The wide and flat grasslands of central Argentina, known as the pampas, are perfect for raising cattle. Cowboys called gauchos work the huge herds that roam the pampas. Many consider the beef of these free-range cattle to be the world's most delicious.

CONNECT THE DOTS

Gauchos were not only daring horsemen, they were also soldiers and a political force in Argentina. Connect the dots to reveal a gaucho in action.

Flag of Argentina

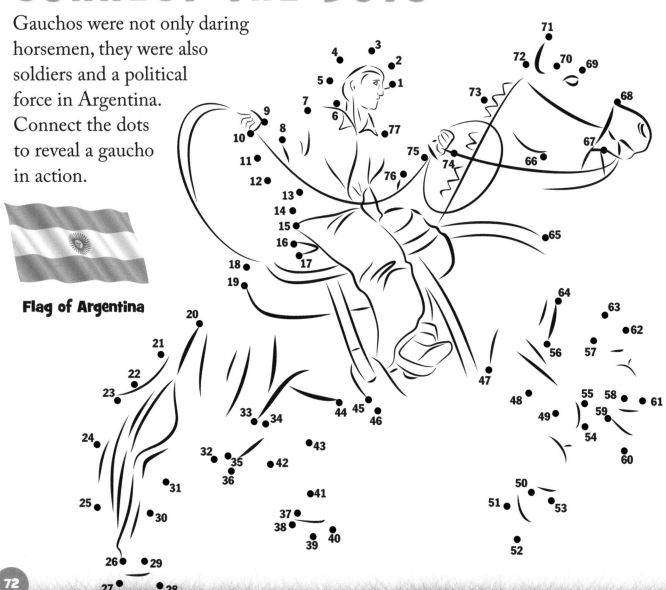

Why was Mohandas Gandhi important to India?

Mohandas Gandhi was born in 1869 in Porbandar, India. The Indian people wanted to end British rule there. Gandhi led non-violent protests, such as fasts and marches, building an independence movement. Gandhi's non-violent methods inspired the world.

ACROSTIC

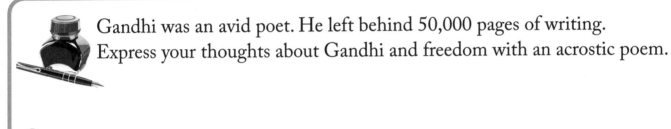

Gandhi was an avid poet. He left behind 50,000 pages of writing. Express your thoughts about Gandhi and freedom with an acrostic poem.

G _____

A _____

N _____

D _____

H _____

I _____

73

History

There's an old saying: "Those who cannot remember the past are doomed to repeat it." People have built amazing societies, accomplished incredible things—and sometimes made terrible mistakes. Studying good and bad moments in history teaches us about our world today.

Teotihuacan

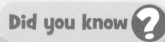

Did you know ?

The holy city of Teotihuacan sits just northeast of Mexico City. It was built between the 1st and 7th centuries A.D. *Teotihuacan* means "the place where the gods were created."

Who was Julius Caesar?

Early in Rome's history, more than two thousand years ago, Julius Caesar rose to power. The general ruled as a dictator. This means he had total authority. Under Caesar's rule, Rome became the center of a great empire. But some Roman senators didn't like rule by dictatorship. Ruled by elected representatives was their goal. Undercover, they plotted to end Caesar's rule. They would have to kill him. Eventually, Marcus Junius Brutus did the deed in 44 B.C., plunging the empire into civil war.

What did Julius Caesar say just before his best friend Brutus killed him?

Use the first letter of every sentence in the paragraph above to construct the sentence.

_ _ _ _ _ _, _ _ _ _ _ _ _?

The words mean, "Even you, Brutus?"

WORD SCRAMBLE

Unscramble the words to find the names of these technologies that originated in ancient Rome.

hgihawy   **aqudeuct**   **sweer sytsem**   **corcnete**

Machu Pichu

Why did the Incas build Machu Picchu?

Archaeologists think this site, 7,970 feet (2430 m) above sea level in the mountains of Peru, served as a royal estate. No one knows how the Incas moved so many massive stones up steep terrain through dense forest. The blocks of stone were cut so precisely that they fit together tightly without mortar.

By the Numbers

El Castillo, a pyramid at Chichén Itzá in Mexico, showcases ancient Mayan mathematics. Its four sides have 365 steps (for each day of the solar year), and 52 panels (for each week in the year).

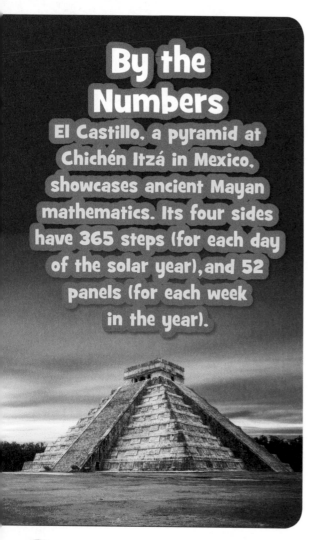

Who was Crazy Horse?

The legendary warrior Crazy Horse (1842–1877) led his first war party when he was still a teenager. For years, he fought off American generals, who wanted to drive the Oglala Lakota off their land. But in 1877, Crazy Horse finally surrendered and was forced onto a reservation. Even in defeat, he held on to his independent spirit. Later that year, he was arrested when he left the reservation without permission to take his sick wife to her family. He was killed during the arrest.

Which American Indian tribe is famous for its rugs?

During the 17th century, the Spanish introduced sheep to the Southwest. The Navajo used wool from the sheep to create rugs. They became known as the best weavers in the region. Most Navajo designs are symmetrical. If you fold them in half, each side is a mirror image of the other.

DRAW AND COLOR

Draw and color the other side of this symmetrical Navajo rug. Then use the space below to create your own.

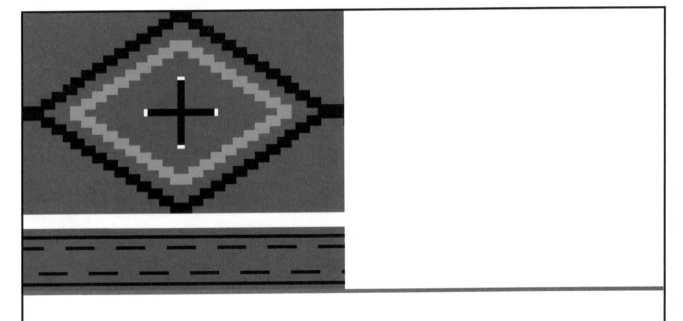

Why is the printing press one of the most important inventions of all time?

Prior to the mid-1400s, making books was a long, hard, and expensive process. Only a few books existed, and only rich people could afford them. That all changed when Johannes Gutenberg of Germany invented the printing press in 1440. The press made it easier to print books, which meant more people could read—and learn.

MAKE A MATCH

Draw a line to match the inventor to his invention.

Nikola Tesla

Orville and Wilbur Wright

Thomas Edison

Charles Babbage

Johannes Gutenberg

Alexander Graham Bell

lightbulb

printing press

mechanical computer

telephone

plane

alternating current electricity

Why did Europeans explore the world?

Christopher Columbus

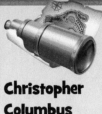

Many European countries sent explorers to find new opportunities for trade, to claim new land, and to search for natural resources such as gold. In 1492, Christopher Columbus set off to find a shorter trade route from Europe to Asia. Instead, he found a new world, which Spain quickly realized could be a source of wealth and power.

CROSSWORD

Complete the puzzle by filling in a word that fits each clue. Write one letter per square.

Across

2. Hernando_____ was the first European to travel west of the Mississippi

3. On his first voyage, in 1492, Columbus set sail from Spain with three ships. They were the Niña, the _____, and the Santa María.

6. In April 1513, Juan Ponce de León landed on the east coast of _____. He claimed the land for Spain.

Down

1. When Columbus landed in the Bahamas in 1492, he thought he had arrived on this continent.

3. Lewis and Clark traveled toward this ocean.

4. A river in New York is named for the English explorer Henry _____.

5. Columbus was from this country.

Why did the Pilgrims come to America?

In their home country, England, Puritans were persecuted for belonging to the English Separatist church. Looking for a place to worship freely, the pilgrims, who were Puritans, set their sights on the New World. They arrived in Plymouth, Massachusetts, in 1620.

Why did the first colony at Roanoke disappear?

A group of English settlers arrived at Roanoke Colony in present-day North Carolina in 1587. By 1590, they had disappeared. Theories about the disappearance range from a deadly disease to a losing battle with Native Americans. Recently, archaeologists have found possible evidence that the missing settlers had actually joined nearby Native American tribes.

Hint: It was the name of an island 50 miles south of Roanoke Colony.

Follow the letters

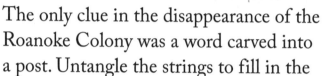

The only clue in the disappearance of the Roanoke Colony was a word carved into a post. Untangle the strings to fill in the blanks and find out what that word was.

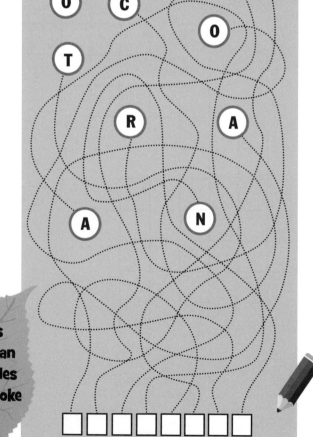

O C O T R A A N

☐ ☐ ☐ ☐ ☐ ☐ ☐ ☐

Why did Paul Revere take his famous midnight ride?

Look at the pictures next to the blanks to figure out what words belong there. Fill in all the blanks to read about Paul Revere.

With revolution brewing, A _ _ _ _ _ _ _ c _ _ _ colonists had stockpiled

 g _ _ n _ _ w _ _ _ and  w _ _ _ _ _ _ _

in Concord, Massachussetts. British troops advanced on the area.

Alerted by  _ _ _ _ i _ s and l _ n _ _ _ _ _ s ,

Paul Revere and William Dawes  r _ _ _ _ horses 20 miles from Boston

to warn the p a _ _ _ _ _ _ t _ . The next day, the first

_ _ _ t _ t _ _ _ _ were fought in Lexington and Concord.

Why was the Declaration of Independence written?

In the years leading up to 1775, England had been making American colonists pay heavy taxes. Anger boiled over, and soldiers and colonists clashed in Massachusetts. After a year of fighting, the Continental Congress agreed to unite the colonies and break with England. Thomas Jefferson drafted a formal document explaining that all men had a right to "life, liberty, and the pursuit of happiness."

Why is Washington, D.C., America's capital?

When the Constitution was ratified, the U.S. capital was in New York City. Then moved to Philadelphia, Pennsylvania. But pro-slavery southern states did not want a capital in the North, where many people were against slavery. The final location was a compromise.

MAZE

Help the president make his way through the maze to the Oval Office.

Why was the Civil War fought?

A group of Southern states seceded, or broke away, from the United States after the election of Abraham Lincoln in 1860. These Southern states thought Lincoln would side with northerners who wanted to abolish slavery. Lincoln was determined to hold the Union together, even if war was the result.

SPOT THE ANACHRONISM

You should find 8!

An anachronism is something that does not belong in the time period in which it is being shown. Circle the items in this Civil War picture that do not belong.

What is Charles Darwin's theory of evolution?

When Charles Darwin published his book *On the Origin of Species* in 1859, it shocked people. In the book, Darwin outlined his theories of natural selection and evolution. He said organisms evolve by inheriting new traits, or characteristics, that allow them to survive and reproduce—a process known as natural selection.

CRISSCROSS

Use words from the word bank to fill in the crossword.

Ancestor   Origin   Theory
Evolution   Species   Trait
Organism   Survive

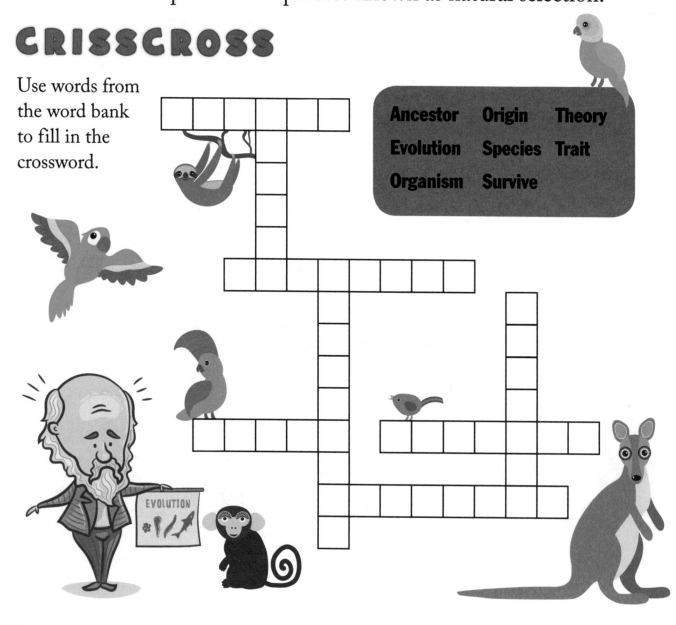

Why was World War I called the War to End All Wars?

In World War I (1914–1918) soldiers from 32 different countries fought throughout Europe. More than 17 million people died, and much of Europe's farms and cities were destroyed. Many hoped it would be the last war ever—"The war to end all wars."

The United States joined the war in 1917 after an intercepted telegram made it clear that Germany was trying to form an alliance with Mexico.

World War I tank

Why did the United States fight in World War II?

When German leader Adolf Hitler started World War II by invading Poland in 1939, many Americans didn't want their country to get involved. But Japan, Germany's ally, wanted to rule the Pacific. Japan bombed Pearl Harbor, Hawaii, on December 7, 1941. The next day, the United States entered the war.

Letter ladder

Follow the lines from MARTIN LUTHER KING, JR., to fill in the names of some of the most important leaders in the civil rights movement. Look at the pictures for clues.

Martin Luther King, Jr.

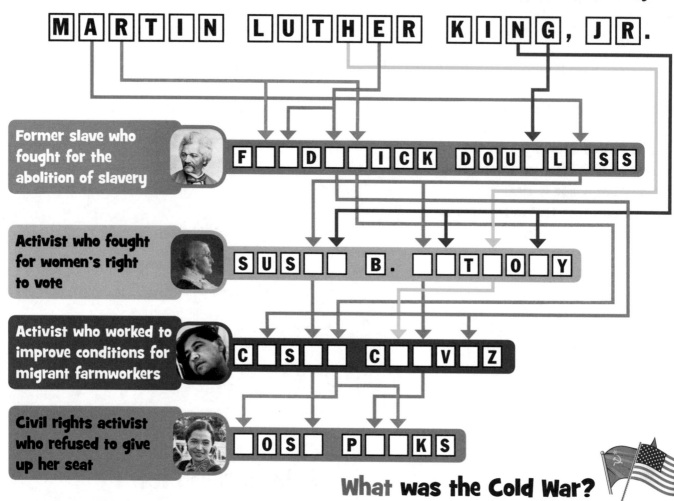

M A R T I N   L U T H E R   K I N G , J R .

Former slave who fought for the abolition of slavery

F □ □ D □ I C K   D O U □ L □ S S

Activist who fought for women's right to vote

S U S □ □   B .   □ □ T □ O □ Y

Activist who worked to improve conditions for migrant farmworkers

C □ S □ □   C □ □ V □ Z

Civil rights activist who refused to give up her seat

□ O S □   P □ □ K S

What was the Cold War?

For almost 50 years following World War II, the U.S. and the U.S.S.R. were bitter enemies. That period is known as the Cold War, because the two enemies never fought directly. The nations spied on each other, and worked to woo other nations to their side to gain power.

Did you know ?

On August 28, 1963, 250,000 people gathered for the March on Washington. They demanded equal rights for people of color.

FUNNY FILL-IN

Without looking at the rest of the sentence, fill in each blank with the type of word listed below it. Then read the whole story to find out how silly it is.

A Sneaky Day

It's 1956, and spying runs in my family. That's why I ended up here, in _____ ,
place

where I can eat all the _____ I want and get some _____ on our enemies.
plural noun   noun

One morning, I _____ , grabbed my _____ , and _____
verb (past tense)   noun   verb (past tense)

to the rendezvous point. I used my _____ to record our _____ . My
noun   noun

informant gave me great _____ about where the _____ was hidden.
noun   noun

He said, "The _____ are _____ and the _____
plural noun   verb ending in "ing"   plural noun

are _____ in _____ ." It was code, and I knew exactly
verb ending in "ing"   place

what it meant. Success! Now it was time for a/an _____ . The next day,
noun

I _____ back to _____ and delivered the _____ .
verb (past tense)   place   noun

My boss said, "Great _____ . You _____ the _____ ."
noun   verb (past tense)   noun

That was code, too. I walked out _____ and _____ .
adjective   adjective

Why was Nelson Mandela's election significant for South Africa?

Beginning in 1948, white people ruled the South African government with a system of laws that kept races separate. This was called apartheid. Nelson Mandela was jailed for 27 years for speaking out against apartheid. In 1990, he was released from prison. He worked with government officials to help end apartheid. And in 1994, under a new constitution, Mandela became the first black president of South Africa.

! This may surprise you . . .

Nelson Mandela's birth name, Rolihlahla, means "troublemaker."

Color this picture of Nelson Mandela.

Why was President Obama's 2008 election historic?

When Barack Obama was elected the 44th president of the United States, he became the first African American to win the nation's highest office. Just four decades earlier, many African Americans were still being denied the right to vote. Obama won more votes than any candidate in U.S. history.

Did you know ?

Obama's heroes are civil rights leaders Martin Luther King, Jr., and Mohandas Gandhi, painter Pablo Picasso, and jazz musician John Coltrane.

Line 'em up!

Can you match these recent presidents with their pictures?

Draw a line between the president's picture and his name!

45. Donald Trump

44. Barack Obama

43. George W. Bush

42. Bill Clinton

41. George H.W. Bush

40. Ronald Reagan

39. Jimmy Carter

Science

Take a moment to look around.
What do you see, smell, or feel?
Science is the study of every aspect
of your physical world through observation
and experiment. What is causing that bad smell?
Why does my soda fizz? How did those clouds form in the sky?
You can find answers to all of your questions through science!

Why does rotting food smell bad?

Food rots when bacteria, mold, and yeasts eat away at it. As these organisms chow down, they give off various gases, which sometimes smell bad.

Why does soda fizz?

Soda makers pump sugared water full of carbon dioxide gas under great pressure. That fizz when you open a soda bottle is the sound of the carbon dioxide molecules bursting free from the liquid.

Why does laundry detergent work?

The most important ingredients in laundry detergent are chemicals called surfactants. One end of a surfactant molecule is attracted to water, and the other end is attracted to dirt and grease. When you put detergent into a washing machine with dirty clothes, the dirt-loving end of the surfactant molecules binds to the dirt. As the water swirls, it pulls the dirt away from the fabric. Dish detergent works the same way on dishes.

A surfactant molecule

This end attracts water.

This end attracts dirt.

Match-up

Which two stains are exactly the same? Circle the match!

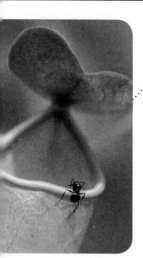

Why do some plants eat bugs?

In some environments, plants cannot get all the nutrients they need from the soil. Certain plants, like the Venus flytrap, developed a solution. Along with food from the soil, these plants evolved to eat bugs. The leaves of the Venus flytrap open wide. When something touches the trigger hairs inside the plant, digestive fluids get to work dissolving the meal.

Feed me, Seymour!

Venus flytraps lure prey with sweet-smelling nectar and also by emitting a fluorescent-blue glow during parts of the day when the light is dim.

It's a trap!

This fly is going to be dinner if she can't get away from the Venus flytrap. Help her find her way out!

Why are there holes in Swiss cheese?

Swiss cheese is made by adding three types of bacteria to milk. As the bacteria eat the milk, two types of bacteria produce lactic acid. The third type of bacteria lives off that lactic acid. As the bacteria eat the acid, they give off bubbles of carbon dioxide, forming the holes.

WORD SCRAMBLE

Different cultures have their favorite cheeses. Some cheeses are only available in the region where they are produced. These are some of the most loved cheeses in America and around the world.

EIRB

_ _ _ _

CDAHEDR

_ _ _ _ _ _ _

TEAF

_ _ _ _

NICEMARA

_ _ _ _ _ _ _ _

ZORGGOONLA

_ _ _ _ _ _ _ _ _ _

GEUERRY

ZALMEOLARZ

_ _ _ _ _ _ _ _ _ _

PREASAMN

_ _ _ _ _ _ _ _

Why are some bacteria good for you?

It's true that some bacteria can make you sick. But other types help keep you alive. Some of those "good" bacteria work inside your body to help you digest food. Other types live on your skin and in your mouth, and protect you against the bad bacteria that can make you sick.

Grossest **WORD SEARCH** Ever

Search up, down, diagonal, backward, and forward and circle the hidden words.

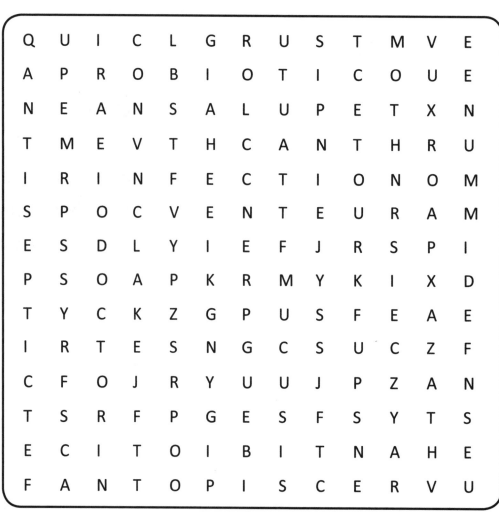

```
Q  U  I  C  L  G  R  U  S  T  M  V  E
A  P  R  O  B  I  O  T  I  C  O  U  E
N  E  A  N  S  A  L  U  P  E  T  X  N
T  M  E  V  T  H  C  A  N  T  H  R  U
I  R  I  N  F  E  C  T  I  O  N  O  M
S  P  O  C  V  E  N  T  E  U  R  A  M
E  S  D  L  Y  I  E  F  J  R  S  P  I
P  S  O  A  P  K  R  M  Y  K  I  X  D
T  Y  C  K  Z  G  P  U  S  F  E  A  E
I  R  T  E  S  N  G  C  S  U  C  Z  F
C  F  O  J  R  Y  U  U  J  P  Z  A  N
T  S  R  F  P  G  E  S  F  S  Y  T  S
E  C  I  T  O  I  B  I  T  N  A  H  E
F  A  N  T  O  P  I  S  C  E  R  V  U
```

antibiotic	bacteria	immune	mucus	pus
antiseptic	doctor	infection	probiotic	soap

Why is composting so good for the planet?

Composting is the process of turning food and yard waste back into rich soil that can grow food, flowers, and other plants. Gardeners who make and use compost are recycling food waste and improving soil quality by adding nutrients.

Sort this garbage!

Cities and towns across the country have put recycling programs into place for households, schools, and businesses. Many have also added curbside composting. So, let's sort this trash! Draw a line from each item to the correct bin.

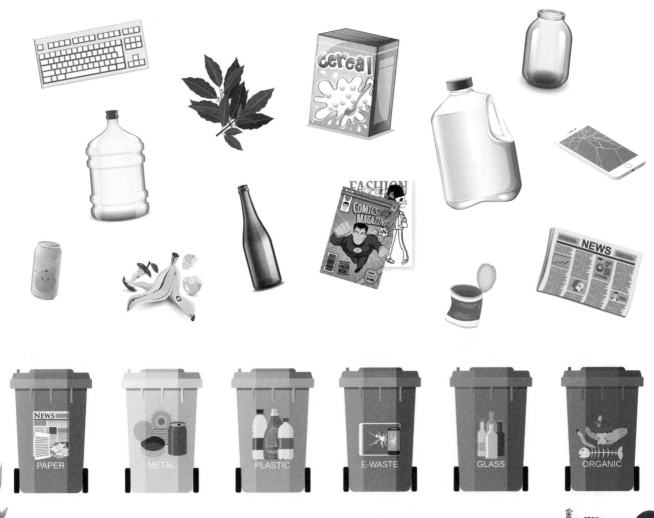

PAPER   METAL   PLASTIC   E-WASTE   GLASS   ORGANIC

Why do baking soda and vinegar explode when mixed?

Vinegar contains acetic acid. When acetic acid reacts with sodium bicarbonate (baking soda), it becomes carbonic acid, which breaks down into carbon dioxide and water. The escaping carbon dioxide gas creates the bubbles you see overflowing like a gushing volcano. Don't do this without permission from an adult!

! This may surprise you . . .

Gunpowder doesn't actually explode. When it burns, the chemicals release gases. However, if the gunpowder is enclosed in a tight space, the gases build up, increasing the pressure in the container. When the pressure gets too great, the container explodes.

Why are fireworks colorful?

Sodium   Copper   Barium   Aluminum

Fireworks are packed with different chemicals. Each chemical produces a particular color when it explodes. Sodium makes fireworks burn yellow or gold. Copper creates blue colors. Barium produces green. And aluminum delivers the ever-popular silver-and-white sparkles.

Pictogram

Look at the pictures next to the blanks to figure out what words belong there. Fill in all the blanks to read about Guy Fawkes.

In the 1600s, many Catholics in E _ _ _ _ _ _ n _ were _ _ g _ y

that the government was persecuting them for their religion. A group of 13 people

decided to _ _ _ _ w _ u _ _ the Houses of Parliament. The assassination

attempt was called the G _ _ n _ _ w _ _ _ Plot. One conspirator,

Guy Fawkes, posed as a caretaker of a cellar below the Houses of Parliament. There,

he and his fellow plotters stockpiled 36 barrels of g _ n _ _ w _ _ _ _.

However, some of the men worried that innocent people might be hurt.

S _ _ l _ _ _ _ _ _ were alerted. On November 5, 1605, Guy Fawkes was

found sitting with _ _ _ t _ h _ _ and his g _ n _ _ w _ _ _.

Today, the _ _ _ g _ _ _ h _ _ c _ _ _ _ b _ _ t _ the

_ _ _ d of the G _ _ n _ _ w _ _ _ Plot on

_ u _ _ _ _ w k _ _ _ Day.

Why does a lightbulb light up?

Every time you turn on an incandescent lightbulb, electricity flows into the bulb, heating a thin coil of metal wire called a filament to an incredibly hot 4,500°F (2,500°C). Hot metal glows brightly. The glass bulb protects the filament and keeps out oxygen—which would make the filament burn too quickly.

Close the circuit!

An electric circuit is a wire pathway through which electrons flow. A power source—such as a battery or a power station—sends voltage that moves electrons along a wire. A light switched "off" creates a gap in the circuit. This stops the flow of electrons. When the switch is turned "on," the gap closes and electricity can travel to power the light.

Lightbulb

Wire

Switch

Battery

Find your way through the lightbulb maze.

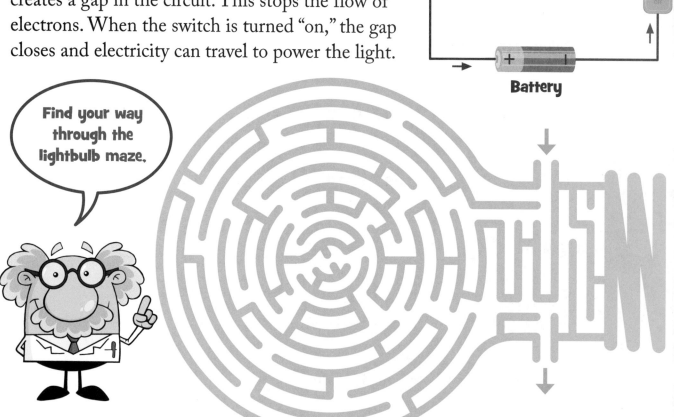

How does a pencil write?

The material inside a pencil is a soft mineral called graphite. As the pencil moves across the paper, tiny bits of graphite rub off, leaving a trail wherever the pencil has gone.

How does an eraser erase?

The friction of rubbing the eraser on paper makes the particles in the rubber stickier than the paper. The graphite particles leave the paper and stick to the eraser instead.

Time for school!

Sam needs to pack his pencil box. Can you find the objects? Trace the outline of each item.

Graphite has been used since the 1500s. Rubber erasers have been used since 1770.

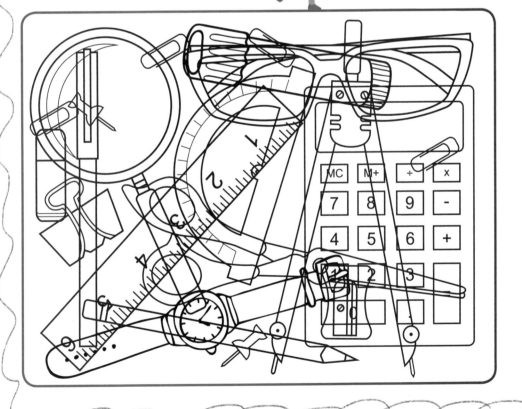

eraser
gluestick
pen
pencil
ruler
scissors
sharpener

Why does snow fall?

A snowflake forms when water vapor attaches to a tiny dust or pollen particle. The water vapor freezes into a hexagon-shaped ice crystal when a cloud's temperature is below freezing (32°F/0°C). If the air temperature between the cloud and the ground is also below freezing, the crystals cling together and fall as snowflakes.

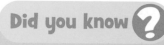
Did you know ❓

As a snowflake falls, it moves through humid air. Water molecules continue to attach themselves to the snowflake in the same hexagonal shape.

Match-up

In a controlled environment, scientists can grow snow crystals that look exactly alike. Can you find the identical snowflakes in this batch?

Why do glaciers move?

The snow that falls on glaciers year after year eventually turns to ice. This process continues for hundreds of years, adding more and more layers on top. All these extra layers add weight. Once these massive slabs of ice become heavy enough, they begin to move. Pressure from all that extra weight causes ice at the bottom of the glacier to melt. The water causes the glacier to slide. Loose soil under the glacier can also cause movement.

! This may surprise you . . .

Glaciers can drastically reshape landscapes over hundreds or thousands of years. They carry away everything in their path, even entire mountainsides! As they retreat or shrink, meltwater or the ocean can fill up the carved basins and troughs.

Land sculptures

These jaw-dropping sites were carved by glaciers.

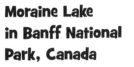

Moraine Lake in Banff National Park, Canada

Glacier Point in Yosemite Valley, California

Green Gardens in Gros Morne National Park, Canada

The Matterhorn, Switzerland

Why do helium balloons float?

Helium is a gas that is lighter than air. A balloon rises because the helium displaces, or pushes away, the heavier air around it. This is known as buoyancy. As the balloon rises into the lower-pressure upper atmosphere, the air in the balloon expands until the balloon pops. Sea creatures, birds, and other animals can choke on deflated balloons, so don't let yours float away.

Why does hot air cause a balloon to rise?

When air is heated, its molecules move faster. The faster the molecules move, the more space they have between them. This means that hot air is less dense than cold air, so the hot air floats on top of the cold air, causing the balloon to rise. The balloon descends as the air inside it cools.

SPOT THE DIFFERENCES

The Albuquerque International Balloon Fiesta is the largest hot-air balloon festival in the world. More than 500 balloons participate. Can you spot and circle ten differences between these two photos?

Keeping score

How many did you you find?

More than 5:
You're on the ball.

More than 7:
You must be eating your carrots.

More than 9:
You're a real eagle eye.

Technology

Through science, math, and engineering, we've been able to create some pretty amazing technology to solve our everyday problems. Technology helps us communicate in an instant clearly and over great distances. It allows us to travel to far-off places quickly and safely. And, for tasks humans can't perform, we've built robots to help!

Why do radio stations have call letters?

When the radio was invented, it was used more like a telephone. Radio operators chose names, numbers, or words to identify themselves. As the number of radio operators increased, so did confusion. The government gave each radio station—and eventually each TV station—its own call letters. West of the Mississippi River, the call letters begin with *K*. Eastern stations begin with *W*.

! This may surprise you . . .

From the 1920s to the 1940s, radio was the main form of entertainment in the United States.
On October 30, 1938, actor Orson Welles shook up the nation with his broadcast of *The War of the Worlds*, a radio drama about a Martian invasion. During breaks, Welles reassured the audience the play was fiction. Still, some listeners thought the invasion was real.

FUNNY FILL-IN

Without looking at the rest of the sentence, fill in each blank with the type of word listed below it. Then read the whole story to find out how silly it is.

War of the Words

Two young _____ see a _____ in the sky. What could it be?

type of animal, plural   noun

_____ : *Hey, did you see that? It looked like a _____!*

Name 1   noun

_____ : *Nah, it wasn't that. I think it was a _____.*

Name 2   noun

_____ : *Ah! I think it's _____! It's going to _____ us!*

Name 1   verb ending in ing   verb

_____ : _____ ! _____ ! *It's landing!*

Name 2   Exclamation   verb

Alien: _____ , _____ ! *Do not be _____ . I do not*

greeting   plural noun   adjective

intend to _____ you. I do, however, want to _____ all of your

verb   verb

_____ . *I've been watching them for _____ light-years. They seem*

plural noun   number

very _____ , and that made me feel very _____ . If you just give me all

adjective   emotion

of your _____ , I won't _____ you, and I will leave in peace.

plural noun   verb

Narrator: **Are all the _____ on Earth doomed? Tune in next week to find out!**

plural noun

01100 10110 11110 Why does binary computer code use ones and zeroes?

The circuits that run computers include many millions of tiny switches called transistors. They can be turned on or off by an electrical pulse. The programs that run computers instantly read those pulses as code. The 1s in computer code turn a transistor on, the 0s turn it off. By creating a long string of 1s and 0s, the program creates words, numbers, commands, and instructions that perform the operations we expect from a computer.

By the Letters

HTTP means hypertext transfer protocol. Those letters tell browsers that what follows will be an address (URL) on the World Wide Web.

http://www.

CROSSWORD

Across

5. Hypertext Transfer _____
6. Surfing tool
7. What @ means
8. Billions of computers linked

Down

1. Code that infects your computer
2. _____ system, also known as OS
3. Another word for computer screen
4. _____ Wide Web
6. This computer code uses ones and zeroes

Internet timeline

1969 — The Advanced Research Projects Agency (ARPA) develops the first computer network.

1971 — Ray Tomlinson creates the first e-mail program.

1981 — The National Science Foundation creates a program that allows computers to connect to each other.

1989 — There are more than 100,000 "hosts," or servers, that hold information other computers can access.

 Sir Tim Berners-Lee creates the World Wide Web. Documents and other Web resources are identified by uniform resource locators, or URLs.

1991 — The first Web browsers allow people to search the Web. Also, Wi-Fi is invented.

1996 — Nokia introduces the first cell phone that can connect to the Internet.

2004 — Nokia introduces the first cell phone that can connect to the Internet.

2006 — Facebook, Twitter, and YouTube are formed to connect people through social media.

 The number of websites on the Web surpasses **1 billion**.

2014

2016 — Almost **2 billion** people use social media.

Why do cars and trucks need gasoline?

Gasoline gives vehicles the power they need to move. Inside the engine, the gas is sparked, causing hundreds of small explosions every minute. Each tiny blast moves the engine's pistons up and down, creating a lot of power. The pistons turn a crankshaft, which moves the vehicle's wheels. Now you're rolling!

DRAW YOUR OWN

Customize your own car! We've drawn the chassis. Now let your imagination run wild with the rest!

A chassis is the base frame of a vehicle.

Why do weird clouds form around supersonic jets?

When an airplane travels slower than the speed of sound, pressure waves move air out of the way before the plane reaches it. But at the speed of sound, an airplane catches up to its own pressure waves and the air has no time to move. The plane knocks air molecules out of the way, creating a shock wave. Pressure, density, and temperature sharply increase among the crowded air molecules. Water vapor in the air heats up and cools in a flash, creating an eerie cloud when a jet approaches supersonic speeds.

Water vapor condenses into a cloud in the shock wave of a supersonic jet.

Fold a plane

You'll need a piece of printer paper or notebook paper. Fold up the edges of the wings, and see if your plane will do a barrel roll. For best results, use a smooth, slow throw.

Fold the paper in half, then open it up again.

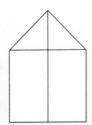
Fold corners down to meet the crease.

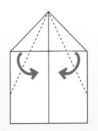
Crease along the edges.

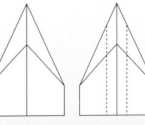
Fold in again to meet the center crease.

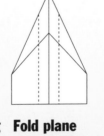
Crease along the edges.

Fold plane in half, then bend down the wings.

Why did the telegraph change the world?

dot   dash

Until the early 1830s, sending a letter was the only way to communicate over long distances. Delivery could take weeks or months. Then, in the mid-1830s, Samuel Morse invented a system that sent electric signals along wires. Using an alphabet made up of dashes and dots—Morse code—those signals could be translated into words. Morse hinted at the power of this new technology in the first message he sent on May 24, 1844.

Use the Morse code key to fill in the letters and read his message.

Be the telegraph operator

A	• ━		N	━ •
B	━ • • •		O	━ ━ ━
C	━ • ━ •		P	• ━ ━ •
D	━ • •		Q	━ ━ • ━
E	•		R	• ━ •
F	• • ━ •		S	• • •
G	━ ━ •		T	━
H	• • • •		U	• • ━
I	• •		V	• • • ━
J	• ━ ━ ━		W	• ━ ━
K	━ • ━		X	━ • • ━
L	• ━ • •		Y	━ • ━ ━
M	━ ━		Z	━ ━ • •

Full stop (period) . • ━ • ━ • ━

Question mark ? • • ━ ━ • •

Did you know

Alexander Graham Bell hoped to build a better telegraph machine that used sound instead of dots and dashes. He finally succeeded by inventing the telephone in 1876.

Can robots improve people's lives?

People who lose limbs can now be helped by robotic prosthetics that connect to their nervous systems. As technology improves, increasingly subtle electrical impulses from a person's body will be received and understood by these sophisticated limbs.

This robotic arm communicates with the brain and allows people who have lost a limb to feel again.

SUDOKU

Fill the empty squares so that the numbers 1 to 9 appear only once in each row, column, and 3x3 box.

3		4	8	6	1		9	2
8	5			4	3	7		1
2		6	5		9		8	4
	9		7	1	5	2		6
5		3		9		1	7	8
1	6	7	3	8			5	9
6	8		4	3	7	9		5
7		2	9	5		8	1	
9	3		1	2		6		7

Your time

Sports

Shoot a basket or a puck. Run the football or the track. Dribble a ball with your hands . . . or your feet. Get moving with the sport of your choice. No matter whether you like to go it alone or on a team—or just watch and cheer—sports can be more than a game.

Flag football is a safer alternative to tackle football.

Tell me a joke **What did the football coach say to the broken vending machine?** "Give me my quarter back!"

Figure it out

Which sport am I?

I am the world's most popular sport.

I have two names.

I am a team sport.

Girls and boys, women and men play me at every level.

Every four years there is a big competition to decide which country is best at me.

SPOT THE DIFFERENCES

Do these two hockey game photos look the same to you? Look again. The original National Hockey League photo is on the top. We made ten changes to the photo on the bottom. Can you spot them all? For an added challenge, time yourself using the timer function on a phone or tablet.

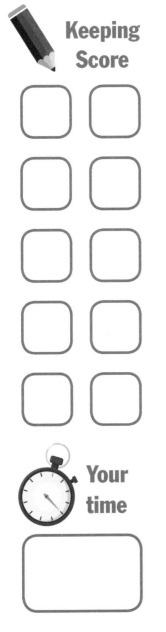

Keeping Score

Your time

Why are rally car drivers considered the best?

Rally car racers drive real cars on real roads—paved and unpaved. They don't find out what the course will be until race day. As a driver speeds along at over 100 miles per hour, a co-driver in the passenger seat uses a route map to warn the driver of the twists and turns ahead. The annual Race of Champions pits NASCAR, Formula One, IndyCar, and rally car drivers against one another in the same type of car on the same course. Rally car drivers have won the most times.

MAZE

Navigate this rally car under and over the bridges to complete the race.

The Monte Carlo Rally is one of the most prestigious races in the world.

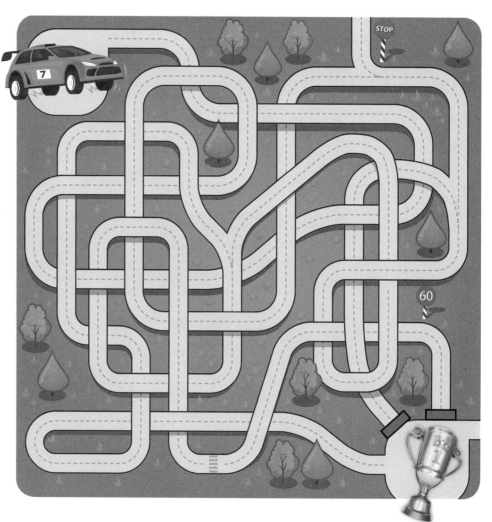

Why does a basketball rim have a net?

A basketball would sail through a rim without a net so fast that officials, players, and fans might miss it. The net is designed to slow down the ball. This way, everyone sees the shot and all points count.

Why is a basketball orange?

Brown basketballs were difficult for crowds to see against wooden floors. College coach Paul "Tony" Hinkle worked with Spalding, a company that made basketballs, to find a brighter color—and just about everyone was seeing orange by 1958.

Connect the dots
Start at one. When you're done, color in a pattern of your choice!

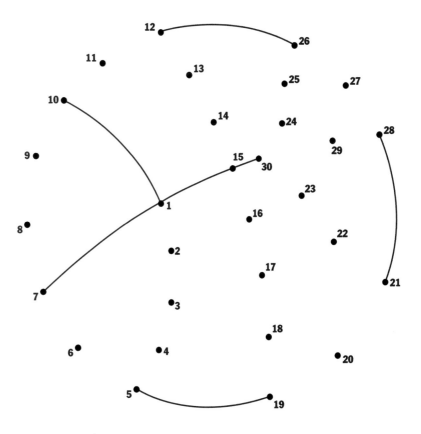

How do soccer players "bend" the ball?

By striking the outside of the ball as they kick it, talented soccer players can put a spin on the ball. This can bend the ball around a wall of players or into a corner of the goal. Kicking with the inside of the right foot bends the ball to the left; using the outside of the same foot bends the ball to the right.

Match-up

Find and circle the two identical soccer balls.

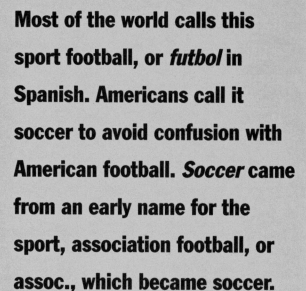

Did you know ❓

Most of the world calls this sport football, or *futbol* in Spanish. Americans call it soccer to avoid confusion with American football. *Soccer* came from an early name for the sport, association football, or assoc., which became soccer.

Why is a touchdown worth six points?

When football began in the late 1800s, kicked goals were more important than touchdowns. As players began doing more running and less kicking, scoring touchdowns became harder. That's why their value increased in 1912 from five points to six. The change was also made to quicken the game's pace.

WORD SEARCH

It's game time! Search up, down, backward, forward, and diagonal for these football terms.

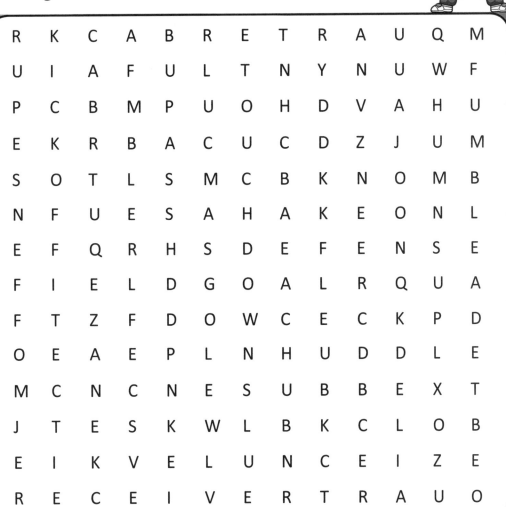

R	K	C	A	B	R	E	T	R	A	U	Q	M
U	I	A	F	U	L	T	N	Y	N	U	W	F
P	C	B	M	P	U	O	H	D	V	A	H	U
E	K	R	B	A	C	U	C	D	Z	J	U	M
S	O	T	L	S	M	C	B	K	N	O	M	B
N	F	U	E	S	A	H	A	K	E	O	N	L
E	F	Q	R	H	S	D	E	F	E	N	S	E
F	I	E	L	D	G	O	A	L	R	Q	U	A
F	T	Z	F	D	O	W	C	E	C	K	P	D
O	E	A	E	P	L	N	H	U	D	D	L	E
M	C	N	C	N	E	S	U	B	B	E	X	T
J	T	E	S	K	W	L	B	K	C	L	O	B
E	I	K	V	E	L	U	N	C	E	I	Z	E
R	E	C	E	I	V	E	R	T	R	A	U	O

Block

Defense

End Zone

Field Goal

Fumble

Huddle

Kickoff

Offense

Pass

Quarterback

Receiver

Tackle

Touchdown

Why did baseball become America's national pastime?

Baseball started as a children's game in the 1700s. But in 1845, a group of men in New York formed the New York Knickerbockers Baseball Club and wrote up the rules of the game. By the 1850s, baseball reporters called it a national pastime, and the title stuck. Baseball is a game that anyone can play and people love to watch. Today, more than 80 million tickets are sold to Major League Baseball games each year.

By the Numbers

A good curveball spins as many as 30 times a second. The most powerful pitchers can throw more than 100 mph.

! This may surprise you . . .

Girls weren't allowed to play Little League Baseball until 1973.

Did you know ?

Right-handed batters often hit better against left-handed pitchers, while lefty batters do well against righty pitchers. Some players learn how to switch-hit, or bat with either hand, always giving them the advantage.

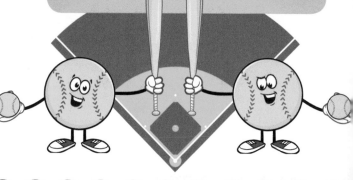

Why do skiers wax their skis?

Skiers and snowboarders (and surfers!) wax their skis and boards to reduce friction. Less friction means more speed!

Find the lost ski!

Janet took a tumble, and now she can't find her skis. Can you find them?

Oops!

In 1965, Sherman Poppen saw his daughter balancing on a single ski in the backyard. It gave him an idea. He put two skis together, called it a snurfer (*snow* + *surf*), and sold it to a toy company—snowboarding was born!

Why are Olympic medals made of different metals?

The tradition of giving medals to winners of Olympic contests began in 1896. The different metals indicated how the contender placed: first-place winners received a silver medal, second took home a bronze, and third-place finishers received nothing. Since 1904, winners have received a gold medal.

Why were the 1936 Berlin Games historic?

The 1936 Games in Berlin, Germany, were held during Adolf Hitler's rule. Hitler's Nazi Party saw non-white races as inferior, and they thought the white Aryan race's superiority would be on display at the Games. But that year, track-and-field athlete Jesse Owens, who was African American, would make history. He won four gold medals, broke or matched nine Olympic records, and set three world records.

Did you know ?

The ancient Olympic Games included some sports that are still played today. Modern Olympic athletes still compete in boxing, equestrian events, discus throw, javelin throw, jumping, running, and wrestling.

Why is there a torch at the Olympic Games?

The flame that burns throughout the Games is a symbol created by the founder of the modern Games, Pierre de Coubertin. For each Olympics, the flame is lit in Olympia, Greece, by the sun's rays. A relay then moves the flame from there to the host city. The first multi-country torch relay was held for the Berlin Games of 1936.

MAZE

Follow the correct route through the maze to connect the Olympian with the sport.

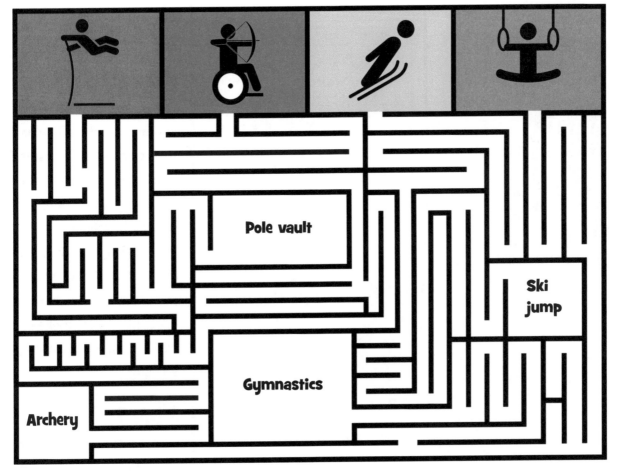

Pole vault

Ski jump

Gymnastics

Archery

Answers

Page 6

ape   monkey   ape

monkey   monkey   ape

Page 9

Spot the difference:

The third crocodile in the row is missing some teeth and a toe!

Page 11

```
          ¹H
²W H I C K E R
          R
          D
        ³S
⁵M A R E T
        A
        L
        L
      ⁶F O A L
        N
```

Page 12

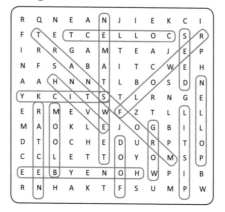

Page 19

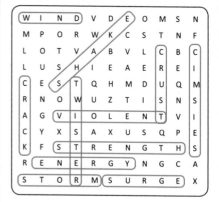

Page 16

Page 13

BALD EAGLE

RAVEN

BARN OWL   SPARROW   ROBIN

BLUE JAY   STARLING

CARDINAL

PELICAN

Page 15

```
R Q N E A N J I E K C I
F T E T C E L L O C S R
I R R G A M T E A J E P
N F S A B A I T C W E H
A A H N N T L B O S D N
Y K C I T S T L R N G E
E R M E V W F Z T L L L
M A O K L E J O G B I L
D T C H E D U Y R T S O
C C L E T O O Y O M S I
E E B Y E N O H W P I B
R N H A K T F S U M P W
```

Page 20

Word scramble:

TORNADO ALLEY

Page 21

Missing words: soda can, gas, explosion, volcanoes, heat, Earth, rock, gases, crust, volcano

Page 23

```
W I N D V D E O M S N
M P O R W K C S T N F
L O T V A B V L C B C
L U S H I E A E R E I
C E S T Q H M D U Q M
R N O W U Z T I S N S
A G V I O L E N T V I
C Y X S A X U S Q P E
K F S T R E N G T H S
R E N E R G Y N G C A
S T O R M S U R G E X
```

Page 27

Energy quiz: Green—cycling, low-energy lightbulb, planting a tree, turning off light switches, electric car, recycling, taking a shower rather than a bath, walking to school

Red—Taking a bath on your own, letting the water run while you brush your teeth, regular lightbulb, driving alone in the car, leaving the bedside light on all night

Page 31

Sink or float?: Sink—rock, metal toy car, coin, pumpkin, plastic dinosaur

Float—Twig, leaf, apple

Page 33

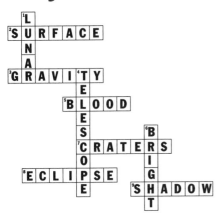

Crossword answers:
1. LUNA (down)
2. SURFACE
3. GRAVITY
4. TELESCOPE (down)
5. BLOOD
6. BRIGHT (down)
7. CRATERS
8. ECLIPSE
9. SHADOW

Page 35

Page 36

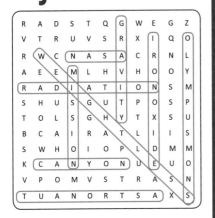

Word search answers include: NASA, RADIATION, CANYON, ASTRONAUT, GRAVITY, OLYMPUS MONS

Page 37

Solar system chart:
MERCURY, VENUS, EARTH, MARS, JUPITER, SATURN, URANUS, NEPTUNE, PLUTO

Answer: GOLDILOCKS PLANET

Page 38

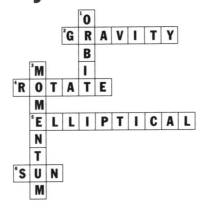

Crossword answers:
1. ORBIT (down)
2. GRAVITY
3. MOMENTUM (down)
4. ROTATE
5. ELLIPTICAL
6. SUN

Page 39

3	9	7	2	8	6	5	4	1
4	1	2	5	3	9	7	6	8
8	5	6	4	7	1	3	2	9
2	8	4	1	9	5	6	3	7
6	3	9	7	4	8	2	1	5
5	7	1	3	6	2	8	9	4
7	2	8	9	1	3	4	5	6
1	6	3	8	5	4	9	7	2
9	4	5	6	2	7	1	8	3

Page 41

Page 42

Word scramble:
ASTEROID BELT

Page 45

Answer: 2,000,000. The average head has about 100,000 hair follicles. Each follicle grows about 20 hairs in a lifetime.

Page 46

Crossword answers:
1. MUCUS (down)
2. BLUE
3. GREEN (down)
4. TEARS
5. BROWN

Page 48

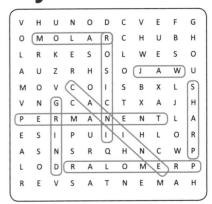

Word search answers include: MOLAR, JAW, PERMANENT, CANINE, ENAMEL

Page 50

Word scramble: SHELLFISH, FISH, MILK, TREE NUTS, WHEAT, EGGS, PEANUTS, SOY

Page 52

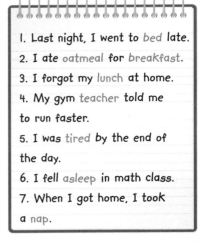

1. Last night, I went to *bed* late.
2. I ate *oatmeal* for *breakfast*.
3. I forgot my *lunch* at home.
4. My gym *teacher* told me to run faster.
5. I was *tired* by the end of the day.
6. I fell *asleep* in math class.
7. When I got home, I took a *nap*.

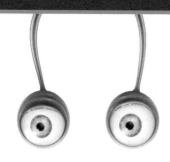

Page 53

Mix and Match:

How do oceans say hello to each other?
They wave!
What do you call cheese that isn't yours?
Nacho cheese!
Why did the math book look so sad? Because it had so many problems!
Why was 6 afraid of 7? Because 7 8 9.
How do you make a tissue dance? You put a little boogie in it.
Why did the picture go to jail? Because it was framed.
Did you hear the joke about the roof? Never mind, it's over your head!

Page 54

Page 60

Page 63

Page 64

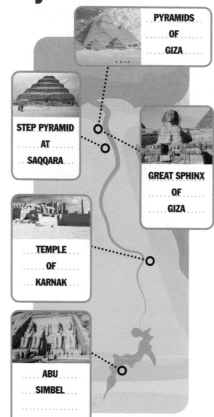

PYRAMIDS OF GIZA

STEP PYRAMID AT SAQQARA

GREAT SPHINX OF GIZA

TEMPLE OF KARNAK

ABU SIMBEL

Page 66 Answer: B, D, E

Page 67
Answer: THE LAND DOWN UNDER

Page 68
Answers: MING, QING

Page 69

Page 75
Answer: ET TU, BRUTE?
Scramble: highway, aqueduct, sewer system, concrete

Page 78
Inventors: Nikola Tesla/alternating current electricity, Thomas Edison/lightbulb, Alexander Graham Bell/telephone, Orville and Wilbur Wright/plane, Johannes Gutenberg/printing press, Charles Babbage/mechanical computer.

Page 79

Crossword:
- 2 DESOTO
- 1 ASIA
- 3 PINTA
- 4 HUDSON
- PACIFIC
- 5 SPAIN
- 6 FLORIDA

Page 80

Follow the letters:

CROATOAN

Page 81

Missing words: American, gunpowder, weapons, spies, lanterns, rode, patriots, battles

Page 82

Page 83

Anachronisms: Jeep (1940), radio (1901), electric guitar (1950), mobile phone (1973), lightbulb (1879), sneakers (1917), headphones (1958), motorcycle (1885)

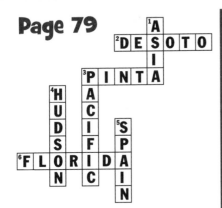

Page 84

Crossword:
- THEORY
- ORIGIN
- ANCESTOR
- EVOLUTION
- SPECIES
- TRAIT SURVIVE
- ORGANISM

Page 86

Letter ladder: Frederick Douglass, Susan B. Anthony, Cesar Chavez, Rosa Parks

Page 89

45. Donald Trump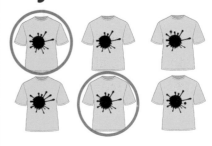

44. Barack Obama

43. George W. Bush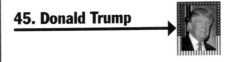

42. Bill Clinton

41. George H.W. Bush

40. Ronald Reagan

39. Jimmy Carter

Page 91

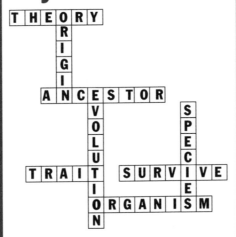

Page 92

It's a trap!:

Paths B and C are safe!

Page 93

Word scramble: BRIE, CHEDDAR, FETA, AMERICAN, GORGONZOLA, MOZZARELLA, GRUYERE, PARMESAN

Page 94

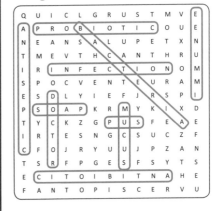

Page 95

Sort this garbage!:

PAPER—Magazines, cereal box, newspaper; METAL—Soda can, tin can; PLASTIC—Water bottle, milk bottle; E-WASTE—Old keyboard, broken mobile phone; GLASS—Green bottle, clear jar; ORGANIC—Garden leaves, fruit peelings

Page 97

Missing words: England, angry, blow up, Gunpowder, gunpowder, Soldiers, matches, gunpowder, British, celebrate, end, Gunpowder, Guy Fawkes

Page 98

Page 99

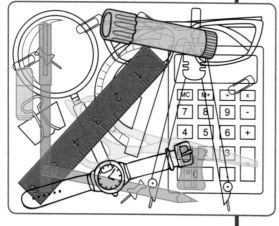

Page 100

Page 103

Page 106

Crossword answers:

1. VIRUS
2. OPERATING
3. MONITOR
4. WORLD
5. PROTOCOL
6. BROWSER
7. ATO
8. INTERNET
BINARY

Page 110

Be the telegraph operator:

What hath God wrought? The message is a quote from the Bible. It means, "What has God made?"

Page 111

3	7	4	8	6	1	5	9	2
8	5	9	2	4	3	7	6	1
2	1	6	5	7	9	3	8	4
4	9	8	7	1	5	2	3	6
5	2	3	6	9	4	1	7	8
1	6	7	3	8	2	4	5	9
6	8	1	4	3	7	9	2	5
7	4	2	9	5	6	8	1	3
9	3	5	1	2	8	6	4	7

Page 112 Figure it out: soccer

Page 113

Page 114

Page 116

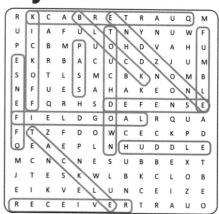

Page 117

```
R K C A B R E T R A U Q M
U I A F U L T N Y N U W F
P C B M P U O H D V A H U
E K R B A C U C D Z J U M
S O T L S M C B K N O M B
N F U E S A H A K E O N L
E F Q R H S D E F E N S E
F I E L D G O A L R Q U A
F T Z F D O W C E C K P D
O E A E P L N H U D D L E
M C N C N E S U B B E X T
J T E S K W L B K C L O B
E I K V E L U N C E I Z E
R E C E I V E R T R A U O
```

Page 119

Page 121

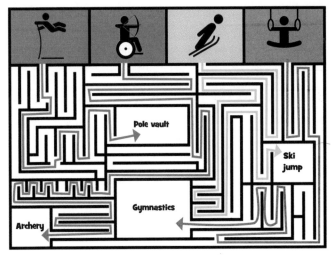

Picture Credits

SS=Shutterstock LOC=Library of Congress GI=Getty Images

Cover front: All images SS—butterfly: boyusya, dot-to-dot: sailorlun, dog photo: steamroller_blues, robot: fresh stock, word search: yavi, kangaroo: Bradley Blackburn, crossword: Ksenya Savva, tornado: Sergey Nivens; **back:** all images: What's my name/SS. **Pages 1:** pencils: WeStudio/SS, **2–3:** All images SS—Fly: Vector Tradition SM, pug: Eric Isselee, Venus: Lorelyn Medina, kids: FoxyImage, green pencil: Gorban, cat: Nikolay Litov, Earth: ixpert, space rocket: MSSA, xray: oculo, Statue of Liberty: dibrova, old map: Natykach Nataliia, scientist: HitToon, www: spreadthesign, basketball player: Cory Thoman; **4–5:** All images SS—blackbird dancing: Nyamol Ds, brown bird: picharyasri, elephant: Dreamcreation, snake: Iconbunny, cat: Pushkin, tiger: Teguh Mujiono, wolf, brown dog, chihuahua: Eric Isselee, Great Dane: Csanad Kiss, mantis art: Insima, mantis photo: nico99, green square: rvika, blackbird: Nyamol Ds, pawprints: Verpeya, pencil: Dacian G, tan dog: Andrey Makurin, boy: graphic-line, gray dog: Red-Spruce; **6–7:** hanging monkey art: drawkman/SS, gorilla: Dreamcreation/SS, plants: Vidoslava/SS, pencil gorilla: Ken Benner/SS, waving monkey: Muhammad Desta Laksana/SS, chimp: Clive Bromhall/Oxford Scientific/Getty, hanging monkey photo: Ingo Arndt/Minden pictures/GI, swinging gibbon: Aku Alip/SS, monkey on branch: LeonP/SS, monkey mom: Anna Kucherova/SS, flower gorilla: photography is my passion and love/GI, orangutan: Jan Kvita/SS, border: Vidoslava/SS, moon: korsaralex/SS, hanging bat: Barsan ATTILA/SS, branch: Mureu/SS, outline bat: Ksenya Savva/SS, flying bat: Pushkin/SS, standing bat: hermandesign2015/SS, **8–9:** shockfactor.de/SS, Boesman's fish: Oliver Lucanus/NiS/Minden Pictures/GI, watery background: Lightkite/SS, fish outline:Hut Hanna/SS, emoji: ober-art/SS, crocodile: defpicture/SS, alligator: Eric Isselee/SS, crocodile: John Kasawa/SS, alligator on log: zeesstof/GI, alligator mom: Andrey Makurin/SS; **10-11:** gray cat: Nikolay Litov/SS, bowl: Yellow Cat/SS, black cat: Teguh Mujiono/SS, orange cat: Pushkin/SS, black cat: Eric Isselee/SS, Grass: iadams/SS, black horse: GraphicsRF/SS, misty horses: Image Source/GettyImages, red rosette: VectorPic/SS, brown horse: Erik Lam/SS, **12–13:** All images SS—tiny ants: Viktorija Reuta, bed, orange ant: Teguh Mujiono, cartoon ant hill: VanDenBlind, ant photo: Andrey Pavlov, ant hill photo: Henrik Larsson, leaf ants: Sonia Goncalves, branch: Kittichai, blue bird: Eloku, black bird: Marcin Perkowski, bald eagle: Serjio74, Owl, sparrow: Eric Isselee, robin: David Spates, starling: Photomaster, pelican: gmstockstudio, cardinal: Charles Brutlag, blue jay: Mike Truchon, leaves: azure1, **14–15:** all images SS—square bees: Darios, bee on flower: Lightspring, smiley: bontom, jar: r.classen, honeycomb: cha cha cha studio; **16–17:** All images SS—orb spider: Stacey Ann Alberts, yellow spiderling: Kletr, gray web: Prikhnenko, brown spiderling: Natabene, black spiders: world of vector, black web: Vladvm, purple firefly: Fer Gregory, yellow bug: Tucker, cartoon fireflies: resnak; **18–19:** all images SS—earth: ixpert, sun: Ksiy1996, Goldilocks: Comodo777, globe with clouds: Inna Biggun, various globes: ideascortes, map: Kaliaha Volha; **20–21:** All images SS—tornado photo: Cammie Czuchnicki, tornado swirl: Macrovector, scuba diver, chicken, frogs, bull, hiker, cartoon tornados: Cory Thoman; exploding volcano background: Ammit Jack, volcano art: Rattanawijittakorn, soda can: Spreadthesign, Erlenmeyer flask: Pavel, explosion: Lightkite, thermometer: stockakia, rock: MSSA, pizza: Anna.zabella, globe: Gruzdev; **22–23:** All images SS—sun: Ksiy1996, Cartoon men: Cory Thoman, snake: Popmarleo, sky: Ezio, grand canyon: Anton Ivanov, temperature gauge: Haryadi CH, rocky border: Alexander Volke, road: Nagadhana, house: Macrovector, cracked road vector: Dolvalol, car: NotionPic; **24–25:** All images SS—sky and sea: ecco, clouds: Garau, seagull: Teguh Mujiono, vector waves: Watchada, Dolphin: Dualororua, waves curve: Longjourneys, tsunami waves: GraphicsRF, beach shack: Vasilyeva Larisa; **26–27:** All images SS—climate globe: kotoffei, umbrella girl: ann131313, rain family: bodom, sunset: Smit, hurricane: Harvepino, ice floes: ribeiroantonio, Fire truck: mikeledray, bear: Mikhel, green house: Aleks47, pencil: createvil, Igloo: Pushkin, penguin: Teguh Mujiono, boy tub: marimariko, cyclists: Lorelyn Medina, eco bulb: FreshPaint, Toothbrush girl: GraphicsRF, tree girl: NotionPic, light switch: momoforsale, electric car: Julia Tim, recycling bin: Photoroyalty, shower kid: Lorelyn Medina, lightbulb: Kraska, walking kids: infoland, bedroom: cate8211, traffic jam: Guaxinim; **28–29:** All images SS—warning sign: Kayser_999, old tree: NotionPic, sphere of stones: Dim Dimich, stone monster: Cory Thoman, Pumice: Richard Roscoe, quarry: Stocktrek Images, Pumice: Rob Kemp, sandstone formations: Jim Parkin, sandstone rock: Alexlukin, marble quarry: Alessandro Colle, marble block: Aleksandr Pobedimskiy, pebble vector repeat: Yoko Design, purple stone repeat: Color Brush, coloured stones repeat: Dacian G, pencil-repeat: BlueRingMedia, **30–31:** All images SS—satellite: dedMazay, comet: Ket4Up, kids on bikes: Lorelyn Medina, Pencil: createvil, plane:3DDock, hot air balloon: corund, cityscape: KID_A, mountain stream: Robert Bohrer, rubber duck: nikiteev_konstantin, pebble: photka, coin: B Brown, toy car: Tatiana Popova, red apple: Tim UR, pumpkin: Jacek Fulawka, dinosaur: AkeSak, leaf: Valentyn Volkov, sdiver: Cory Thoman, Bathtub: Direnko Kateryna, Waves: vector21kompot; **32–33:** proto Earth: NASA, rocket, astronaut with flag: MSSA/SS, Milky Way: Denis Belitsky/SS, Asteroid: Vadim Sadovski/SS, Moon: godrick/SS, blood moon: Chris Collins/SS, full moon: Alhovik/SS, kid: Sean Locke Photography/SS; **34–35:** space rocket: 3Dsculptor/SS, game pieces: Jackie Nishimura/SS, waving astronaut: MSSA/SS, astronaut, telescope, space station, galaxy, orbits, stars, comet, satellite: Alexander Ryabintsev/SS, exclamation: SVStudio/SS, space rocket icon: Olegro/SS, storm: Aleksii/SS, colored rockets: VectorA/SS, ISS: NASA, satellite: Firuz Salamzadeh/SS, woman astronaut on a rocket: Lucky clover/SS, maze: Fir4ik/SS, Earth: owatta/SS; **36–37:** Martian landscape: Andrii Stepaniuk/SS, Alien eyes: Lonely/SS, Mars: NASA/JPL-CALTECH, Martian landscape2: Andrii Stepaniuk/SS, solar system: Bildagentur Zoonar GmbH/SS, Pluto: Jut/SS, pencil: createvil/SS; **38–39:** galaxy: Marina Sun/SS, globes: Twin Design/SS, Milky Way NASA/JPL-Caltech/R. Hurt (SSC/Caltech), planets cartoon: Minur/SS, Spaceship: Algol/SS, sudoku puzzle: Khaladok/SS, moon landing: Castleski/SS; **40–41:** elliptical galaxy: QAI Publishing/GI, sun: NASA's Goddard Space Flight Center/SDO/S. Wiessinger, spiral galaxy: NASA, ESA, and the Hubble Heritage (STScI/AURA)-ESA/Hubble Collaboration, dwarf galaxy: ESA/Hubble & NASA, star border: Rena Design/SS, laughing emoji: ober-art/SS, spaceship: MSSA/SS, alien: Studio G/SS, planet earth vector: Art Alex/SS; **42–43:** comet: MSSA/SS, calendar: Jane Kelly/SS, green alien: Visual Generation/SS, asteroid belt: NASA/JPL-Caltech, asteroids: festa/SS, pluto and Charon: NASA/Johns Hopkins University Applied Physics Laboratory/Southwest Research Institute, pencil: createvil/SS, sun icon: Ksiy1996/SS, spaceship: MSSA/SS; **44–45:** faces, doctors: KanKhem/SS, Skin: karalak/SS, yellow hairbrush: VectorPlotnikoff/SS, red hairbrush: accurate shot/SS, girl with curly hair: Flashpop/GI, pencil-repeat: createvil/SS, squiggle: Filimonova/SS, face outline: Katerina Davidenko/SS; **46–47:** two friends: JenniferPhotographyImaging/GI, outline man: NLshop/SS, brown eyes: Markus Gann/SS, green eyes: argus/SS, blue eyes: PandaWild/SS, brown eyes2: newelle/SS, tired child: narikan/SS, various eyeballs: siridhata/SS, color blindness test: eveleen/SS, broccoli: 13Imagery/SS, crying emoji: Jovanovic Dejan/SS, injured boy: BlueRingMedia/SS, girl: ankomand/SS; **48–49:** All images SS—girl with tooth: kikoo, false teeth: lalan, tooth & brush: Maharani, toothfairy: revidevi, row of teeth: MoonRock, pencil: createvil, girl whistling: Paula Ohreen, funny face: monoo; **50–51:** All images SS—allergic reaction: Lorelyn Medina, funny lobster, peanut butter man : Cory Thoman, eggs: Evan Lorne, shellfish: Iryna Denysova, peanuts: Hong Vo, tree nuts: rio, wheat: ddsign, milk: Somchai Som, soy beans: domnitsky, fish: Africa Studio, cartoon peanuts: SM, strong bone: kotikoti, skeleton cartoon: VectorHills, bones: VectorHills; **52-53:** All images SS—sleeping boy: Hung Chung Chih, Moon: Alhovik, clouds: wonlopcolors, notebook: Velchev, boy at desk: NotionPic, sleepy emoji: Yayayoyo, alarm clock: stockshoppe, laughing emoji: ober-art, kids: suerz; **54–55:** All images SS—food label: Derek Hatfield, fruit: Giraffarte, gingham pattern: tribalium, plates: Sudowoodo, egg: Brazzik, puzzle food: Skokan Olena, cheese: Donnay Style, chocolate: ArtMari, choc egg: egg design, various chocolates and cupid: kappacha, rows of chocolates: Krushevskaya; **56–57:** freckly face: world of vector/SS, hands: Todd Kuhns/SS, short basketball player: Ron Leishman/SS, tall basketball player: Ron Leishman/SS, painted handprints: Sushko Anastasia/SS, Seurat painting: DEA Picture Library/GI, picture frame: Sanin/SS, country scene outline: Carla Francesca Castagno/SS; **58–59:** All images SS—group of kids: Lorelyn Medina, Burj Khalifa: EschCollection, globe with landmarks: sdecoret, flags in spheres: dikobraziy, Tower of Pisa photo: Fedor Selivanov, Italian girl: pichayasri, Tower of Pisa cartoon: Vectorshots, Grass: iadams, two workmen: Iconic Bestiary; **60–61:** Mount Kilimanjaro: wallix/SS, hiker: Malchev/SS, female hiker: Cory Thoman/SS, mountain maze: tetiva/SS, flags in spheres: dikobraziy/SS, Everest: Vixit/SS, K2: Punnawit Suwattananun/SS, Aconcagua: Santiago Urquijo/GI, Golden Gate bridge: Luciano Mortula-LGM/SS, city scene: itVega/SS; **62–63:** Flags: Mzinchenko/SS, Statue of Liberty repeat: dibrova/SS, Statue of Liberty cartoon: Cory Thoman/SS, pencil: Dacian G/SS, 3D pointers: wormig/SS, map of world: kowition/SS, girl jumping: KanKhem/SS, Statue of Unity: Anand Purohit/Getty images, Spring Temple Buddha: Zgpdszz/Creative Commons, Ushiku Daibatsu: MIXA/GI, Motherland Calls: Zhukov Oleg/SS, Christ the Redeemer: Catarina Belova/SS, little house: alexmstudio/SS, plinth: WRU Party/SS; **64–65:** All images SS—great pyramids: Pius Lee, stepped pyramid: Rhianna Brandon, sphinx: Don Mammosser, Karnak: Waj, Abu Simbel: Ivanov, map of Egypt: Panda Vector, Ancient Egyptian guy: Cory Thoman, ancient map: Jose Ignacio Soto, hieroglyphs: artform, Hagia Sophia: muratart, Sultan: Cory Thoman, Hagia Sophia: Dmitri Mikitenko, Arabic border pattern: Malysh Falko; **66–67:** All images SS—Russian church: Nchutchikov, funny onion: Zhe Vasylieva, jigsaw outline: DVARG, St. Basil's Cathedral: Vladitto, Russian dolls: notkoo, map of Australia: Creativector, kangaroo: Andrey Makurin, Aborigines: ChameleonsEye, koala: Nadzin; **68–69:** All images SS—lion statue: GOLFX, picture frame: Wisaad, Forbidden City: Brian Kinney, panda: sundatoon, terracotta soldiers: mary416, dragon: lunokot, cherry blossom: Lora Sutyagina, jumping schoolgirls: KanKhem, cherry blossom park: IamDoctorEgg, duck: nkula, pencil: Dacian G., Japanese Kokeshi Dolls: Gavrilova; **70–71:** boy with camera: Lorelyn Medina/SS, giant turtle: Kkulikov/SS, blue-footed booby: Tui de Roy/Minden Pictures/GI, Darwin's finch: Adalbert Dragon/SS, pencil: createvil/SS, Moai heads art: Artur Balytskyi/SS, Moai heads photo: Kunst/SS, girl standing: suerz/SS, grass: iadams/SS, fseal: GraphicsRF/SS, iguana: curiosity/SS, bird vector: haibo li/SS; **72–73:** boy: KanKhem/SS, gouchos: Phillip Lee Harvey/Getty images, flag: Magcom/SS, horserider: art3/SS, grass: Dima Moroz/SS, girl with flag: stockillustration/SS, pen-and-ink: Tetiana Yurchenko/SS, kids holding hands: i_sedano/SS, Gandhi: AFP/Getty Images; **74–75:** war pilot: What's My Name/SS, Abe Lincoln: Tomacco/SS, roman archer: Fun Way Illustration/SS, Egyptian: asantosg/SS, Teotihuacan: Dmitri Rukhlenko/SS, pattern: Isaac Zakar/SS, Julius Caesar statue: T.Fabian/SS, Ancient Greek guy: Amplion/SS, pencil-repeat: Dacian G/SS, Roman soldier: Fun Way Illustration/SS, Roman highway: WitR/SS, aqueduct: Bertl123/SS, sewer system: Mondadori Portfolio/GI, Roman basilica: Javen/SS; **76–77:** Inca: Nicholas Greenaway/SS, Machu Picchu: saiko3p/SS, horseman: Steinar/SS, Chichen Itza: Fer Gregory/SS, Crazy horse statue: Smith Collection/Gado/GI, Navajo blanket weaver: LOC, pencil: G/SS, red pencil: Flipser/SS, navajo pattern:Olga Tagaeva/SS, navajo border: Axi/SS; **78–79:** Gutenberg and press: Sipley/ClassicStock/GI, girl with book: Olga1818/SS, Nicola Tesla: LOC, girl in wheelchair: Medina/SS, reading kids: Lorelyn Medina/SS, Thomas Edison: Everett Historical/SS, Alexander Graham Bell: LOC, Gutenberg: Everett Historical/SS, Wilbur Wright: LOC, Orville Wright: LOC, Charles Babbage: LOC, lightbulbs: Ezume images/SS, printing press: Dja65/SS, mechanical computer: Science Photo Library/GI, telephone: Everett Historical/SS, Wright plane: LOC/Digital version by Science Faction/GI, AC Electricity: brunOrbs/SS, books on shelf: Verkhozina Ekaterina/SS, piles of books: Malchev/SS, Christopher Columbus: LOC, map and telescope: Natykach Nataliia/SS, seagull: Teguh Mujiono/SS, coins: sumire8/SS, explorer ship: Kozyreva Elena/SS, sea vector: MicroOne/SS; **80–81:** pilgrims cartoon: Pushkin/SS, arrival of pilgrims: school/GI, knife: Jeff Wilber/SS, corn: Vextok/SS, Roanoke Mountain: Brm Reusen/SS, swirl leaves: paprika/SS, gold leaf: ekler/SS, pencil: Dacian G/SS, quilt pattern: tandaleah6/SS, moon: Alhovik/SS, rider: Leremy/SS, colonial flag: Seth E. Gallmeyer/SS, gunpowder: Olha Zinovatna/SS, cannon: burstfire/SS, gun: JRMurray76/SS, spy: Tomacco/SS, lantern: Crisan Rosu/SS, rider: Ash/SS, patriots: Tomacco/SS, Battle scene: SuperStock/GI, George Washington: Tomacco/SS; **82–83:** Washington: Its design/SS, Lincoln: Tomacco/SS, maze: jelisua88/SS, oval office: pantid 123/SS, stars and stripes border: america365/SS, magnifying glass kid: ankomando/SS, Civil War soldiers: National Archives/Stocktrek Images/GI, lightbulb: 24Novembers, iphone: tmpr/SS, jeep: LandFox/SS, guitar: Mindscape studio/SS, radio: Billion Photos/SS, sneakers: Everything/SS, motorbike: Kitiphong Pho/SS; **84–85:** Charles Darwin: Everett Historical/SS, parrot, sloth, small bird, monkey: EkaterinaP/SS, red parrot: Elena Kazanskaya/SS, cockatoo, kangaroo, crocodile, platypus: Elena Kazanskaya/SS, Darwin cartoon: Yeti Crab/SS, WWII soldiers: Everett Historical/SS, WWI tank: Historical/SS, Pearl Harbor ship: Archive Holdings Inc/GI, cartoon soldier: Julien Tromeur/SS, WWII truck: Svinkin/SS, WWII tank: Svinkin/SS; **86–87:** Martin Luther King: SuperStock/GI, Frederick Douglass: LOC, Susan B. Anthony: LOC, Cesar Chavez: William James Warren/GI, Rosa Parks: National Archives, Russian flag: Tribalium/SS, Flag: SLdesign/SS, snowy detail: Artram/SS, spy figure running: Leremy/SS, chain break: Nobelus/SS, chains: Abree/SS, spy with briefcase: MSSA/SS, top secret stamp: ducu59us/SS, spy peeking: Studio_G/SS; **88–89:** Mandela: Alessia Pierdomenico/SS, boy with SA flag: robbylokamp/SS, kids with flags: curiosity/SS, African pattern: Axusha/SS, SA flag outline: Iznodesign/SS, Nelson Mandela outlined: Dario Mitidieri/GI, Obama: LOC, Uncle Sam: Cory Thoman/SS, George HW Bush: Adrian Dennis/GI, Reagan: David Hume Kennerly/GI, Clinton: Joseph Sohm/SS, Carter: Nir Levy/SS, Trump: Joe Seer/SS, George W Bush: Joseph August/SS, Obama: Action Sports Photography/SS, stars and stripes frame: nalinn/SS, donkey and elephant: RedKoala/SS; **90–91:** child scientist: Lorelyn Medina, garbage bag: andriano.cz, stinky sandwich, Lorelyn Medina, gas bubbles: Szasz-Fabian Jozsef, soda cans: Altagracia Art, bottles of pop: Regina F. Silva, bubbles border: Oxy_gen, washing machine: Antonova Elena, funny scientist: HitToon, bubbles and water background: Vjom, stain splats: Lightkite, tee shirt: dofmaster; **92–93:** pitcher plant: Thilanka Perera/GI, fly: Vector Tradition SM/SS, Venus flytrap: Hayati Kayhan/SS, banana peel: larryrains/SS, Venus flytrap: Lorelyn Medina/SS, apple core: petovarga/SS, green leaves: Lara Govorit/SS, cheese factory: Stephano Ember/SS, Swiss cheese: Valentyn Volkov/SS, camel: BlueRingMedia/SS, Edam cheese: Iconic Bestiary/SS, Brie: gresei/SS, French flag: Anatoly Tiplyashin/SS, Cheddar: Hue Ta/SS, Union Jack: charnsitr/SS, Feta: Moving Moment/SS, Greek flag: bekulnis/SS, American cheese: MSPhotographic/SS, US flag: charnsitr/SS, Gorgonzola: Only Fabrizio/SS, Italian flag: Anatoly Tiplyashin/SS, mozzarella: Tanya Sid/SS, Gruyere: Murat Tegman/SS, Swiss flag: Gil C/SS, parmesan: Ailisa/SS; **94–95:** All images SS—green slime: Sunflower, bacteria cartoons: robuart, earthworm: nalin chanthorn, compost heap: Andrei Verner, kids: Lorelyn Medina, keyboard: drawforLife, bay leaves: Oksana Alekseeva, cereal box: GraphicsRF, glass jar: La Gorda, plastic bottle: TrifonenkoIvan, green bottle: Macrovector, bw magazine: yusuf doganay, comic magazine: benchart, soda can: AltagraciaArt, food waste: petovarga, milk carton: BlueRingMedia, iphone: mvp_stock, tin can: GraphicsRF, newspaper: Tetiana Yurchenko, waste bins: DRogatnev, plant: Jaroslav Machacek, worm in earth: nalin chantho; **96–97:** All images SS—science kids: Lorelyn Medina, volcano experiment: busypix, gunpowder barrels: Tribalium, yellow and blue fireworks: Nasgul, green fireworks: Zeynep Demir, silver fireworks: Mod-X, firework border: stockshoppe, fireworks: Gino Santa Maria, UK map: Aelius Aaron, angry face emoji: ober-art, explosion icon: MSSA, gunpowder and barrels: Olha Zinovatna, soldier: Saranai, matches: Paket, Union Jack: naslizart, celebration icon: Macrovector, stop sign: loftystyle, Guy Fawkes: Donkeyworx; **98–99:** All images SS— lightbulb: Kraska, circuit: Jakinnboaz, scientist: HitToon, maze: Wisaad, string lights: Angela Jones, pencil closeup: Kucher Serhil, eraser: Picsfive, boy: kotikoti, funny pencil: Notionpic, gluestick outline: Hagra, watch outline: maljuk, stationery outlines: bsd, **100–101:** All images SS—snowy border: Vjom, girl: Yuliya Evstratenko, snowman: rvika, snowflakes: Kichigin, Yegor Larin, Alexey Kljatov, Alexey Kljatov, adventurers: Fun Way Illustration, glacier: Dmitry Trashchenko, Moraine Lake: Zhukova Valentyna, Green Gardens: Wildnerdpix, Matterhorn: evenfh, Glacier Point: topseller; **102–103:** All images SS—boy with balloon: IgorAleks, balloons: koya979, Bluebird, pigeon: Nyamol Ds, balloon lit: manlio_70, balloons border: Dawn Hudson, Pencil: Dacian G, balloon festival: Aneese, airplane: badahos, Hanglider: Alexandra Lande, seagull: Passakorn Umpornmaha, kite: stable, boy with binoculars: brgfx; **104–105:** kids with gadgets: What's My Name/SS, radio transmitter: Tribalium/SS, studio: Inti St Clair/GI, Welles: CBS Photo Archive/GI, book cover: Universal History Archive/GI, technology icons, Vlad Rudniy/SS, spacecraft, Qiun/SS, microphone: Epsicons/SS, Alien waves: Visual Generation/SS; **106–107:** All images SS—binary code: Botond1977, WWW: alphaspirit, laptop robot: Vikasuh, computer kids: Lorelyn Medina, laptop: Christos Georghiou, motherboard: Magnia, hipster: Visual Generation, running computer: penguinline, email emoji: Yayayoyo, vintage computer: Stephen Rudolph, mouse: Yayayoyo, WWW: Spreadthesign, wifi computer: Usagi-P, phone guy: Bplanet, computer kids: Lorelyn Medina, social media icons: Rose Carson, surprised boy: Victor Brave, social media: Studio_G; **108–109:** All images SS—gas pump: Sergii Tverdokhlibov, engine: Nikonaft, black, red, and green hot rod: Allex77B, orange hot rod: Mechanik, driver: Cory Thoman, chassis: Nerthuz, flames: squarelogo, sonic boom: SVSimagery, plane outlines: bounward, boy: Ron Leishman, paper plane instructions: Atmosphere1; **110–111:** smiling girl: Nyamol Ds/SS, desk: Nyamol Ds/SS, morse decoder: Ensuper/SS, old phone: gallofoto/SS, morse code: Laralova/SS, robotic arm: St Louis Post-Dispatch/GI, robot: Vikasuh/SS, stopwatch: Blast/SS, puzzled robot: Vikasuh/SS, robots: cgterminal/SS, other robots: Spring Bine/SS; **112–113:** hockey girl: KanKhem/SS, baseball kid: KanKhem/SS, football kid: KanKhem/SS, lightbulb: Sunspire/SS, tag football: Gary Paul Lewis, laughing emoji: ober-art, sports balls: nalinn/SS, starry background: Marina Sun/SS, pencil: Dacian G/SS, ice hockey: Dave Sandford/SS, stopwatch: On Blast/SS, hockey player: Stanislav Ratushnyi/SS, **114–115:** winner: Klara Viskova/SS, tire marks: pingebat/SS, rally car: PODIS/SS, trophy: Alex Mit/SS, maze: Savgraf/SS, stopwatch: Dragance137/SS, rally race: Jean Pierre Clatot/Stringer/GI, checker pattern: Icons vector/SS, basketball in net: Lane V Erickson/SS, girl with basketballs: FoxyImage/SS, basketball game: Aspen Photo/SS, basketball graphics: Svetlana Maslova/SS; **116–117:** soccer photo: Sergey Peterman, soccer cartoon: bazzier, soccer ball: schwarzhana, world soccer: gualtiero boffi, soccer graphic1: Vector Tradition SM, soccer graphic2: thaikrit, soccer graphic3: ArtDesignIllustration, soccer players: Monkey Business Images, various soccer icons: Macrovector, football player: Tomacco, touchdown: peepo/SS, football icons: Cory Thoman, football cartoons: Deus Casus; **118–119:** All images SS—baseball player: Cory Thoman, curve ball: Purematterian, baseball pitcher: Aspen Photo, kid player: BlueRingMedia, cartoon baseball: HitToon, baseball pitch: Oleksandr Yuhlchek, skier: Lukas Godja, snowboarder: Alexey Grigorev, snowsurf: anigoweb, snow chalets: Lorelyn Medina, ski jumper: Artstada, skiiers: didiaCC, tree: alexokokok, dog: Lana_Samcorp, red and blue skiers: Iryna Dobrovynska, pink skier: MatoomMi, skiing family: Lorelyn Medina, snowman: Pinar Ince, trees: SofiaV, sledder and skiers: uiliaaa; **120–121:** Olympic medals: The Asahi Shimbun/GI, runner: aurielaki/SS, Paralympian: AnutaBerg, Jesse Owens: Print Collector/GI, Greek vase: Leemage/GI, Grecian: AnutaBerg, Olympic icons: NataliaProkofyeva, Olympic torch: Vasilis/SS, Olympic flag: Mihai Dud/SS, athlete: Thoman/SS, pole-vaulter, ski-jumper, gymnast: browndogstudios/SS, archer: Macrovector/SS, maze: Milena Moiola/SS; **122:** suerz/SS; **128:** kids: suerz/SS.